Conservation and Management of the Living Marine Resources of Fire Island National Seashore
(Fire Island National Seashore Science Synthesis Paper)

Technical Report NPS/NER/NRTR—2005/023

David O. Conover, Robert Cerrato, and William Wise

Marine Sciences Research Center
Stony Brook University
Stony Brook, New York 11794-5000

December 2005

U.S. Department of the Interior
National Park Service
Northeast Region
Boston, Massachusetts

The Northeast Region of the National Park Service (NPS) comprises national parks and related areas in 13 New England and Mid-Atlantic states. The diversity of parks and their resources are reflected in their designations as national parks, seashores, historic sites, recreation areas, military parks, memorials, and rivers and trails. Biological, physical, and social science research results, natural resource inventory and monitoring data, scientific literature reviews, bibliographies, and proceedings of technical workshops and conferences related to these park units are disseminated through the NPS/NER Technical Report (NRTR) and Natural Resources Report (NRR) series. The reports are a continuation of series with previous acronyms of NPS/PHSO, NPS/MAR, NPS/BSO-RNR and NPS/NERBOST. Individual parks may also disseminate information through their own report series.

Natural Resources Reports are the designated medium for information on technologies and resource management methods; "how to" resource management papers; proceedings of resource management workshops or conferences; and natural resource program descriptions and resource action plans.

Technical Reports are the designated medium for initially disseminating data and results of biological, physical, and social science research that addresses natural resource management issues; natural resource inventories and monitoring activities; scientific literature reviews; bibliographies; and peer-reviewed proceedings of technical workshops, conferences, or symposia.

Mention of trade names or commercial products does not constitute endorsement or recommendation for use by the National Park Service.

This report was accomplished under Cooperative Agreement 1443CA4520-99-007, modification #38, with assistance from the NPS. The statements, findings, conclusions, recommendations, and data in this report are solely those of the author(s), and do not necessarily reflect the views of the U.S. Department of the Interior, National Park Service.

Print copies of reports in these series, produced in limited quantity and only available as long as the supply lasts, or preferably, file copies on CD, may be obtained by sending a request to the address on the back cover. Print copies also may be requested from the NPS Technical Information Center (TIC), Denver Service Center, PO Box 25287, Denver, CO 80225-0287. A copy charge may be involved. To order from TIC, refer to document D-127.

This report may also be available as a downloadable portable document format file from the Internet at http://www.nps.gov/nero/science/.

Please cite this publication as:

Conover, D.O., R. Cerrato, and W. Wise. December 2005. Conservation and Management of the Living Marine Resources of Fire Island National Seashore (Fire Island National Seashore Science Synthesis Paper). Technical Report NPS/NER/NRTR—2005/023 National Park Service. Boston, MA.

NPS D-127 December 2005

PREFACE

FIRE ISLAND NATIONAL SEASHORE
Science Synthesis Papers to Support Preparation of a
General Management Plan

BACKGROUND AND PURPOSE

Fire Island National Seashore (FIIS) is scheduled to begin preparation of a new General Management Plan (GMP) in the near future. A GMP outlines how natural and cultural resources, public uses, and park operations should be managed over the next several decades. The GMP addresses significant issues or challenges that are facing the park, proposes management solutions, and establishes management priorities. The Fire Island GMP will be prepared by a team of planners, with input from the park, technical subject matter experts, and with substantial public involvement.

To insure that the GMP team has all relevant natural resource information available to them, a series of scientific synthesis papers has been prepared for a variety of natural resource topics that will be of special relevance to the Fire Island GMP. Based on a 2-day meeting with the FIIS Superintendent, FIIS Chief of Natural Resource Management, Northeast Region planners, and Northeast Region science staff, the following natural resource topic areas were identified;
- Geomorphology of beaches and dunes
- Physical processes of the bay shoreline
- Habitat ecology and water quality of Great South Bay
- Conservation of Living Marine Resources (habitats, finfish and shellfish)
- Vector-borne diseases
- White-tailed Deer ecology and management

For each of these topics, leading scientific experts were invited to prepare papers that synthesize our current state-of-knowledge. There is a wealth of published technical information on these topics. The purpose of these papers was to provide a scientifically credible summary of the available and relevant information and present this information in a succinct manner. The GMP team will receive papers that provide an objective, independent and expert synthesis of an extensive and often complex technical literature. Each paper was subject to the scientific peer review process.

Each synthesis paper is expected to accomplish the following;
- Synthesize and interpret the relevant literature and monitoring data to describe the fundamental processes controlling the natural resource, and describe historic and recent trends or rates of change for relevant processes, habitats, or species.
- Describe current and historic management, regulatory, and other activities that have been relevant to the particular natural resource.
- Identify gaps in our current understanding of the natural resource.

Because the synthesis papers are prepared prior to initiation of the GMP process, if information gaps are considered critical to decision-making for the GMP there may be adequate time to conduct the appropriate required studies or data analysis tasks. Moreover, the papers will serve to identify topics or issues that should be the focus of additional synthesis or review papers in support of the GMP information gathering and synthesis phase.

OVERVIEW OF THE PAPERS

These summaries are derived, with some editing, directly from the individual papers.

The Coastal Geomorphology of Fire Island: a Portrait of Continuity and Change
Technical Report NPS/NER/NRTR—2005/021
Authors: Norbert P. Psuty, Michele Grace, and Jeffrey P. Pace
                  Rutgers University

Summary: Fire Island has a well-developed beach on the ocean side and is dominated by a variety of dune features, reaching elevations of 11-13m. Much of the island is undeveloped and retains a wide array of coastal dune forms in near natural condition. However, there are a number of residential communities, primarily on the western portion of Fire Island, that have altered the landscape and geomorphological processes. The controlled inlets at either end of the island are a type of interactive feature that have particular roles in the passage of sand along the shore. Thus, the geomorphological characteristics and configuration of the island are products of a suite of natural processes, complemented by human actions. This paper describes the landforms (beaches, dunes, inlets, and barrier island gaps) and basic controls on these landforms, such as tides, wave climate, storm history, the availability and rate of supply of sediment, and sea level rise.

There is insufficient sediment coming to Fire Island from all of the potential sources to maintain the entire system. There is evidence of erosion on all parts of the island, except the artificially-created Democrat Point. The sediment deficits are greatest along the eastern portion of the island, but are buffered in the central and western area because of the contributions from an offshore source. The recent acceleration in sea-level rise, coupled with the general negative sediment budget, will result in continued beach erosion and dune displacement, with greater effects occurring in the eastern portion of the island.

During the peer review process, it was determined that a follow-up synthesis paper should be prepared that specifically focuses on the response of Fire Island beaches and dunes to human activities, including ORV traffic, structures, sand fencing, beach scraping, and other activities. This paper is presently being developed.

Bay Shoreline Physical Processes, Fire Island
Technical Report NPS/NER/NRTR—2005/020
Authors: Karl F. Nordstrom, Rutgers University
                  Nancy L. Jackson, New Jersey Institute of Technology

Summary: Wave and current energies on the bay side of Fire Island are low, but much of the bay shoreline is eroding. The greatest changes occur near inlets or next to marinas and bulkheads. Inlets, overwash and dune migration deliver sediment from the ocean to the bay where it forms substrate that evolves into tidal flats, marshes and beaches. These sediment inputs allow barrier islands to maintain themselves as they migrate landward under the influence of sea level rise. The creation and migration of inlets in the past extended their influence well beyond locations of present inlets.

About 17.0 km of the 49.5 km long bay shoreline of Fire Island is marsh; 24.5 km is beach; and 8.0 km is fronted by bulkheads, marina breakwaters and docks. The biggest constraints to allowing Fire Island to undergo natural dynamism are the desire to protect private properties on the island from erosion and overwash and the need to protect the mainland from flooding due to formation of new inlets. Bulkheads are common on the bay shore in developed communities. These structures replace natural formations landward of them and prevent sand from entering the littoral drift system, causing sediment starvation in unprotected areas downdrift. These adverse effects can be reduced by replacing lost sediment by beach nourishment. Use of beach fill on the low tide terrace covers benthic habitat. This problem could be avoided by placing fill above the mean high water mark, creating an eroding feeder upland.

Dune building projects on the oceanside and construction of bulkheads on the bayside restrict the delivery of sediment by inlets, wave overwash and aeolian transport. Temporary inlets would provide some sediment, but artificial closure by human efforts would limit these inputs to a much smaller area than in the past.

Future sea levels are expected to rise at a greater rate, causing increased frequency of overwash and creation of new inlets if not prevented by beach nourishment and dune-building projects on the oceanside. Elimination of the delivery of sediment to the bayside by these natural processes will result in continued retreat of the bay shoreline into the higher portions of the barrier island, resulting in loss of marsh habitat, increase in open water habitat, and truncation of cross-shore environmental gradients.

Water Quality and Ecology of Great South Bay
Technical Report NPS/NER/NRTR—2005/019
Author: Kenneth R. Hinga
            University of Rhode Island

Summary: The overall objective of this paper is to present a short synopsis of information on the characteristics of water quality and ecology of the Great South Bay, with particular attention to the waters within the boundaries of Fire Island National Seashore (FIIS), where possible. This report serves as an update and addition to the report *Estuarine Resources of the Fire Island National Seashore and Vicinity* (Bokuniewicz et al., 1993). Great South Bay is approximately 45 km long, with a maximum width of about 11 km. The Bay is shallow, with an average depth at mean low water of just 1.3m.

Regarding water quality, a review of bacterial indicator monitoring data suggests that some bayside beaches and marinas of Fire Island have had fecal coliform concentrations that are at or approaching levels of concern, but in general the levels are quite acceptable. Nutrient enrichment is an issue for all shallow, enclosed, lagoon-type estuaries, like Great South Bay. There is an encouraging trend of decreasing dissolved inorganic nitrogen in Great South Bay over the past quarter century. Coincident with the decline in nitrogen, there appears to be a trend of decreasing primary production, as determined by measuring phytoplankton chlorophyll concentration, over the past 15 years. Historically, portions of Great South Bay (e.g., near and in Moriches Bay) experienced intense phytoplankton blooms, probably attributed to discharges from duck farms. Since 1985, a brown tide has occurred periodically to disruptive levels in the Bay. Brown tide blooms can cause significant mortalities of hard clams and can damage seagrass beds because the blooms prevent light sufficient to support growth of the seagrass species. The densest seagrass beds in the Bay are found along the shallow shoreline of the Seashore.

Conservation and Management of Living Marine Resources
Technical Report NPS/NER/NRTR—2005/023
Authors: David O. Conover, Robert Cerrato, and William Wise
              Stony Brook University

Summary: The finfish species likely to be landed by commercial harvesters from Fire Island NS or nearby waters are bluefish, winter flounder, summer flounder, weakfish, Atlantic silversides, and menhaden. The recreational species landed within the Bay have not been described in detail since the 1960s, but total recreational landings for New York as a whole suggest that fluke, winter flounder, bluefish, weakfish, tautog, and black sea bass are the main species. Some of the fish species landed in the Seashore region are present only transiently as older juveniles and adults. Such species would include striped bass, menhaden, eels, and weakfish. These species do not use the Bay as a spawning and nursery area. Other species use Fire Island waters as both nursery grounds for young-of-the-year (YOY) stages as well as adults. The value of Seashore estuarine habitats for these species is great (bluefish, winter flounder, fluke, tautog, black sea bass). Ecologically important species, those that are an important forage species for piscivorous fishes, include Atlantic silversides, bay anchovy, sand lance, northern pipefish, and others. Killifishes are a major component of the fish fauna of salt marsh habitats. Shellfish of potential recreational or commercial value found within Seashore boundaries include surfclam, hard clam, blue mussel, soft clam, oyster, bay scallop, razor clam, conch, blue crab, Jonah crab, rock crab, lady crab, spider crab, and horseshoe crab (although not technically classified as shellfish). Generally, there has been a dramatic decline in the commercial harvest of shellfish species from the Bay. For example, since 1976 the harvest of hard clams has declined 100 fold. It is recommended that the Seashore take a leadership role in reaching out cooperatively to government and non-government agencies toward encouraging restoration of Great South Bay living marine resources and increasing public awareness of coastal zone management issues.

Vector-borne Diseases on Fire Island
Technical Report NPS/NER/NRTR—2005/018
Author: Howard S. Ginsberg
              USGS-Patuxent Wildlife Research Center

Summary: This paper discusses eleven tick-borne and five mosquito-borne pathogens that are known to occur at FIIS, or could potentially occur. The potential for future occurrence, and ecological factors that influence occurrence, are assessed for each disease. Lyme disease is the most common vector-borne disease on Fire Island. The Lyme spirochete, *Borrelia burgdorferi*, is endemic in local tick and wildlife populations. Public education, personal precautions against tick bite, and prompt treatment of early-stage infections can help manage the risk of Lyme disease on Fire Island. The pathogens that cause Human Monocytic Ehrlichiosis and Tularemia have been isolated from ticks or wildlife on Fire Island, and conditions suggest that other tick-borne diseases (including Babesiosis, Rocky Mountain Spotted Fever, and Human Granulocytic Ehrlichiosis) might also occur, but these are far less common than Lyme disease, if present.

West Nile Virus (WNV) is the primary mosquito-borne human pathogen that is known to occur on Fire Island. Ecological conditions and recent epizootiological events suggest that WNV occurs in foci that can shift from year to year. Therefore, a surveillance program with appropriate responses to increasing epizootic activity can help manage the risk of WNV transmission on Fire Island.

White-tailed Deer Ecology and Management on Fire Island
Technical Report NPS/NER/NRTR—2005/022

Author: H. Brian Underwood
               USGS-Patuxent Wildlife Research Center

    Summary: Deer populations have grown dramatically on Fire Island National Seashore (FIIS) since 1983. Trend data reveal a dichotomy in deer dynamics. In the eastern half of the island, deer density appears to have stabilized between 25-35 deer/km^2. In the western half of the island, deer densities are 3-4 times as high in residential communities. Concomitant with that increase has been a general decline in physical stature of some animals, visible impacts on island vegetation, especially in the Sunken Forest, and a perceived increase in the frequency of human and deer interactions. Intensive research on FIIS has shown that deer occupy relatively predictable home ranges throughout the year, but can and do move up and down the island. Impacts of deer on vegetation are most dramatic in the Sunken Forest. Most obvious are the effects of browsing on the herb layer of the Sunken Forest. The least obvious, but perhaps more significant impact is the stark lack of regeneration of canopy tree species since about 1970, which coincides with the initiation of the deer population irruption. A number of herbs and shrubs have been greatly reduced in the understory, and their propagules from the soil.

    Deer do not readily transmit the bacterium that causes Lyme disease to other organisms, but deer are important hosts for adult ticks which underscores their importance in the transmission pathway of the disease to humans. Deer on FIIS, while occasionally docile, are still wild animals and should be treated as such. Some animals are relatively unafraid of humans due to the absence of predation and a lack of harassment. This in turn has contributed to a long-standing tradition of feeding deer by many residents and visitors, particularly in western portions of the island. Feeding affects both the behavior and population dynamics of deer inhabiting Fire Island. Recent efforts to reduce deer feeding by visitors and residents have been very effective. Ongoing experiments with Porcine Zona Pellucida immunocontraception demonstrate some promise of this technology as a population management tool. Success appears to be linked directly to factors affecting access to deer, which vary considerably among treatment locations. Continued high National Park Service visibility among communities in the form of interpretive programs, extension and outreach activities, and continued support of research and monitoring of deer and their effects on island biota are keys to successful resolution of persistent issues.

Preface prepared by:
Charles T. Roman
National Park Service
North Atlantic Coast Cooperative Ecosystem Studies Unit

TABLE OF CONTENTS

INTRODUCTION

The Fire Island National Seashore (FIIS) is beginning the process of preparing a new General Management Plan (GMP) to guide the management of the park's natural and cultural resources, visitor activities, and park operations. The park's boundaries encompass the nearshore waters of the Atlantic Ocean and Great South Bay (GSB). These marine and estuarine environments support a diverse assemblage of living marine resources (LMR's) and the habitats upon which these resources depend. By LMR's, we primarily mean those marine organisms that are of particular economic, recreational, ecological, or charismatic value; those that are rare; and the essential habitats of these species. Historically, FIIS has not actively managed the submerged portion of its property (i.e., below the high tide line), yet the marine areas of the Park are substantially larger than its land area. Human population growth and development in the coastal zone are dramatically increasing nationwide. With the recognition that we must manage and protect ecosystems, not just individual species, the need for strategic plans encompassing both the terrestrial *and* marine components of National Park Service units is clear. LMR's and human activities affecting these resources should be an important element of the GMP.

The purpose of this paper is first to describe the LMR's of FIIS in terms of individual key species, essential habitat, and as part of the larger Great South Bay and Mid-Atlantic Bight ecosystems. Second, we describe the history and present status of commercially and recreationally harvested species, the extent to which these activities have occurred within the vicinity of Fire Island, and the potential impact these activities might have on LMR's. Third, we describe the various government agencies, programs, and environmental groups that play a regulatory or advisory role in the management of the GSB and adjacent mid-Atlantic region, and with which FIIS will cooperate during the GMP process. Finally, we suggest and outline an LMR management plan for the Seashore, including: general goals and objectives; potential management actions; a strategy for implementation; and research and monitoring efforts that will be needed to ensure the success of, and adaptively improve, the management plan before and after implementation.

Before preparing this report, we convened a meeting of representatives of federal, state and local agencies and non-governmental organizations having at least partial jurisdiction over some portion of the marine resources of GSB. The goal was to foster an open dialogue about the manner in which FIIS might contribute constructively and synergistically with other agencies in managing and protecting the LMR's of the south shore region. This meeting was held on 24 March 2004 at Stony Brook University. The input of these officials was incorporated into our recommendations but the views expressed herein are those of the authors and not the agencies or the National Park Service.

GENERAL DESCRIPTION OF THE FIIS/GREAT SOUTH BAY ECOSYSTEM

Fire Island National Seashore includes 42 km of Fire Island and 25 small nearby islands within Great South Bay. On land, the park has a diversity of terrestrial areas ranging from accessible, mixed-use areas with communities to the Otis Pike High Dunes Wilderness Area, the only federally designated wilderness area in New York State. The National Park Service

1

boundary extends from mean high water (MHW) 4000 feet into GSB and 1000 feet into the Atlantic Ocean. Within these boundaries, there are four major marine habitats: intertidal beaches/flats, salt marshes, non-vegetated subtidal areas, and vegetated subtidal areas.

Shellfish and benthos: habitats and species

Intertidal beaches/flats - - Intertidal beaches and flats occur along the entire length of the ocean shoreline of FIIS and along the portion of the bay shoreline not occupied by salt marsh vegetation. Few studies have been made of this habitat. Steinback (1999) conducted an extensive seasonal study of the macroinvertebrate communities at six exposed ocean beach sites within FIIS. Samples were taken along the entire width of each beach. Within the intertidal zone, the dominant species were the polychaete *Scolelepsis squamata*, the mole crab (*Emerita talpoida*), and the haustoriid amphipods *Amphiporeia virginiana* and *Haustorius canadensis* (Steinbeck 1999) (Table 1). Croaker (1970) sampled intertidal ocean and bay beaches primarily along Long Island's south shore and Peconic Bay. Four of his 17 sampling locations were located within or near FIIS, but his report does not provide results by station. The common fauna listed by Croaker (1970) are listed in Table 1.

Salt marshes - - There are no published studies of salt marsh fauna within FIIS. The faunal assemblage probably includes benthic species common in the subtidal, along with several species endemic to marshes. The endemic species include the ribbed mussel (*Geukensia demissa*), the mud snail (*Ilyanassa obsoleta*), and the fiddler crabs (*Uca pugilator*) and (*Uca pugnax*) (Table 2). There is some harvesting of green crabs (*Carcinus maenas*) and fiddler crabs (*Uca* spp.) for bait in the south shore bays (SSER 1999), but it is unknown whether this occurs within the FIIS.

Non-vegetated, subtidal areas - - The south shore of Long Island supports a diverse benthic fauna and flora both within and outside the boundaries of Fire Island National Seashore. The fauna differ in composition between ocean and bay primarily because of differences in sediments, salinity and temperature ranges, and hydrographic regime. On the ocean side, several U.S. Army Corps of Engineers funded studies have sampled the benthic fauna at or near potential sand borrow areas south of FIIS (Cerrato 1983, National Park Service 2003, U.S. Army Corps of Engineers 2004). In all of these studies, grab samples were collected at stations 0.5 to 1.5 miles off Fire Island in water 30 to 60 feet deep. Although these sampling locations are beyond the boundary of FIIS, the fauna are likely to be representative of the ocean bottom within the park. Descriptions of faunal community structure in all of these studies are fairly similar and representative species are listed in Table 3.

The benthic fauna on the bay side has been characterized in a number of studies conducted in Great South Bay and Moriches Bay (O'Connor 1972, Marine Sciences Research Center 1973, WAPORA Inc. 1982, Cerrato 1986, Wiggins 1986, and Larson 2000). Very little of the sampling for these studies was carried out within FIIS, and the fauna adjacent to the former Bluepoints Company property has never been examined. Within FIIS, bay sediments are primarily sandy. Combining the results of the existing studies, two distinguishable species assemblages are present: a high salinity ($\geq$ 28), high flow fauna associated with the inlets (Fire Island and Moriches) and a second, lower salinity fauna. Common species are listed in Table 3.

<u>Vegetated, subtidal areas</u> - - The infaunal community of vegetated, subtidal areas is similar to that found in unvegetated subtidal flats, based on grab sample data obtained by O'Connor (1972), Marine Sciences Research Center (1973), WAPORA (1982), and Cerrato (1986). Little information is available on epifauna, since they are not collected efficiently by grab. Raposa and Oviatt (2000) collected larger decapod species in throw traps along the north shore of Fire Island. Common decapods included sand shrimp (*Crangon septemspinosa*), shore shrimp (*Paleomonetes pugio*), grass shrimp (*Hippolyte pleuracanthus*), and blue crab (*Callinectes sapidus*) (Table 4). All four species were more abundant in seagrass beds than on unvegetated sand flats. Seagrass beds are probably important nursery grounds for blue crabs, although no data are available for Great South Bay.

Table 1. Common benthic species of intertidal beaches/flats. Functional group codes are interpreted as follows. First character: I = infaunal and E = epifaunal. Second character: T = tube-building and N = nontubiculous. Third character: M = motile and S = sessile. Last characters: C = carnivore, Di = infaunal deposit feeder, Ds = surface deposit feeder, O = omnivore, S = suspension feeder. Phylum, Class, Family, and Species are given unless otherwise noted.

Taxa	Functional Group	Distribution/ Abundance	Source
Annelida			
Polychaeta			
Nephtyidae			
Nephtys bucera	INMC	near FI inlet	Croker (1970)
Nereididae			
Nereis arenaceodonta	INMO	near FI inlet	Croker (1970)
Orbiniidae			
Haploscoloplos fragilis	INMDi	near FI inlet	Croker (1970)
Spionidae			
Scolelepis squamata	INMDi	ocean beach/FI inlet	Croker (1970) Steinbeck (1999)
Mollusca			
Bivalvia			
Myidae			
Mya arenaria	INSS	bay flats	NONE
Veneridae			
Mercenaria mercenaria	INSS	bay flats	NONE
Arthropoda			
Amphipoda (Order)			
Haustoriidae			
Acanthohaustorius millsi	INMDi	near FI inlet	Croker (1970)
Neohaustorius biarticulatus	INMDi	near FI inlet	Croker (1970)
Amphiporeia virginiana	INMDi	ocean beach	Steinbeck (1999)
Haustorius canadensis	INMDi	ocean beach	Steinbeck (1999)
Isopoda (Order)			
Chaetiliidae			
Chiridotea coeca	ENMO	near Jones Inlet	Croker (1970)
Chiridotea nigrescens	ENMO	near Jones Inlet	Croker (1970)
Decapoda (Order)			
Hippidae			
Emerita talpoida	INMO	ocean beach	Steinbeck (1999)

Table 2. Common benthic species of salt marshes. Functional group codes are interpreted as follows. First character: I = infaunal and E = epifaunal. Second character: T = tube building and N = nontubiculous. Third character: M = motile and S = sessile. Last characters: C = carnivore. Di = infaunal deposit feeder, Ds = surface deposit feeder, O = omnivore, S = suspension feeder. Phylum, Class, Family, and Species are given unless otherwise noted. n/a = not available.

Taxa	Functional Group	Distribution/ Abundance	Source
Mollusca			
Gastropoda			
Ellobiidae			
Melampus bidentatus	ENMO	n/a	NONE
Littorinidae			
Littorina littorea	ENMO	n/a	NONE
Nassariidae			
Nassarius obsoletus	ENMO	n/a	NONE
Bivalvia			
Mytilidae			
Geukensia demissa	INSS	n/a	NONE
Arthropoda			
Decapoda (Order)			
Sesarmidae			
Sesarma reticulatum	ENMO	n/a	NONE
Ocypodidae			
Uca pugilator	ENMDs	n/a	NONE
Uca pugnax	ENMDs	n/a	NONE
Portunidae			
Carcinus maenas	ENMO	n/a	NONE

Table 3. Common benthic species in non-vegetated subtidal areas. Functional group codes are interpreted as follows. First character: I = infaunal and E = epifaunal. Second character: T = tube building and N = nontubiculous. Third character: M = motile and S = sessile. Last characters: C = carnivore. Di = infaunal deposit feeder, Ds = surface deposit feeder, O = omnivore, S = suspension feeder. Phylum, Class, Family, and Species are given unless otherwise noted.

Taxa	Functional Group	Distribution/ Abundance	Source
Annelida			
Polychaeta			
Polygordiidae			
Polygordius triestinus	INSDs	ocean	USACE (2004)
Ampharetidae			
Asabellides oculata	ITSDs	ocean	USACE (2004)
Magelonidae			
Magelona riojai	INMDs	ocean	USACE (2004)
Nephtyidae			
Nephtys picta	INMC	bay near Moriches Inlet	Cerrato (1986)
Nereididae			
Nereis arenaceodonta	INMO	bay near Moriches Inlet	Cerrato (1986)
Sabellariidae			
Sabellaria vulgaris	ETSS	abundant in Patchogue Bay	Wiggins (1986)
Spionidae			
Spiophanes bombyx	INMDi	ocean	USACE (2004)
Terebellidae			
Trichobranchus glacialis	ETSDs	abundant in Patchogue Bay	Wiggins (1986)
Mollusca			
Gastropoda			
Calyptraeidae			
Crepidula fornicata	ENSS	bay near inlet?	NONE
Cylichnidae			
Acteocina canaliculata	ENMC	dominant in Patchogue Bay	Wiggins (1986)
Melongenidae			
Busycotypus canaliculatus	ENMC	Significant predator of large clams	WAPORA (1982)
Bivalvia			
Mactridae			
Mulinia lateralis	INSS	dominant in Patchogue Bay	Wiggins (1986)
Spisula solidissima	INSS	ocean	USACE (2004)

Table 3 (continued)

Taxa	Functional Group	Distribution/ Abundance	Source
Mytilidae			
Mytilus edulis	ENSS	bay near inlets Moriches- biomass dominant	Cerrato (1986) O'Connor(1972)
		bay near inlet abundant	WAPORA (1982) MSRC (1973)
		common food organism of GSB fishes	MSRC (1973)
Ostreidae			
Crassostrea virginica	ENSS	commercial species	NONE
Pharidae			
Ensis directus	INMS	commercial species	NONE
Tellinidae			
Tellina agilis	INSDs	bay near inlet Moriches- biomass dominant	Cerrato (1986) O'Connor (1972)
		abundant in Islip only ocean	WAPORA (1982)
			USACE (2004)
Veneridae			
Gemma gemma	INSS	Moriches- biomass dominant	O'Connor (1972)
		dominant in Brookhaven	WAPORA (1982)
Mercenaria mercenaria	INSS	abundant in Patchogue Bay	Wiggins (1986)
		Moriches- biomass dominant	O'Connor (1972)
Arthropoda			
Amphipoda (Order)			
Corophiidae			
Corophium tuberculatum	ETMS	abundant in Patchogue Bay	Wiggins (1986)
Haustoriidae			
Protohaustorius wigleyi	INMDi	ocean	USACE (2004)
Gammaridae			
Gammarus annulatus	ENMO	ocean	USACE (2004)
Aoridae			
Pseudunciola obliquua	ETMDs	ocean	USACE (2004)

Table 3 (continued)

Taxa	Functional Group	Distribution/ Abundance	Source
Merostomata			
Limulidae			
Limulus polyphemus	ENMC	abundant in Brookhaven	WAPORA (1982)
Malacostraca			
Mysidae			
Neomysis americana	ENMO	principal food source for summer flounder	Poole (1964)
Decapoda (Order)			
Crangonidae			
Crangon septemspinosa	ENMO	bay & ocean- food source for summer flounder	Poole (1964)
		ocean	Cerrato (1983)
Paguridae			
Pagurus longicarpus	ENMO	bay near inlet	WAPORA (1982)
Portunidae			
Callinectes sapidus	ENMO	not abundant in 1978	WAPORA (1982)
		principal food source for summer flounder	Poole (1964)
		common food organism of GSB fishes	
			MSRC (1973)
Ovalipes ocellatus	ENMO	bay near inlet	WAPORA (1982)
		common food organism of GSB fishes	MSRC (1973)
		ocean	Cerrato (1983)
Tanaidacea (Order)			
Tanaidae			
Leptognatha caeca	ITMDs	ocean	USACE (2004)
Echinodermata			
Asteroidea			
Asteriidae			
Asterias forbesi	ENMC	bay near inlet	WAPORA (1982)
Echinoidea			
Echinarachnidae			
Echinarachnius parma	INMDi	ocean	USACE (2004)

Table 4 . Common benthic species of vegetated subtidal areas. Functional group codes are interpreted as follows. First character: I = infaunal and E = epifaunal. Second character: T = tube building and N = nontubiculous. Third character: M = motile and S = sessile. Last characters: C = carnivore. Di = infaunal deposit feeder, Ds = surface deposit feeder, O = omnivore, S = suspension feeder. Phylum, Class, Family, and Species are given unless otherwise noted.

Taxa	Functional Group	Distribution/ Abundance	Source
Annelida			
Polychaeta			
Oenonidae			
Arabella iricolor	INMO	abundant	MSRC (1973)
Capitellidae			
Heteromastus filiformis	INMDi	abundant in Moriches	Cerrato (1986)
Lumbrineridae			
Lumbrineris brevipes	INMO	abundant	MSRC (1973)
Lumbrineris tenuis	INMO	abundant	Cerrato (1986)
		abundant	MSRC (1973)
Maldanidae			
Clymenella torquata	ITMDi	biomass-dominant	O'Connor (1972)
		abundant	MSRC (1973)
Nephtyidae			
Nephtys picta	INMC	common	Cerrato (1986)
Nereididae			
Nereis arenaceodonta	INMO	common	Cerrato (1986)
Neanthes virens	INMO	biomass-dominant	O'Connor (1972)
Neanthes succinea	ITMDs	dominant	MSRC (1973)
Platynereis dumerilii	INMO	dominant	MSRC (1973)
Orbiniidae			
Haploscoloplos fragilis	INMDi	dominant	MSRC (1973)
Sabellidae			
Demonax microphthalmus	ETSS	abundant	MSRC (1973)
Spionidae			
Prionospio heterobranchia	ITMDs	abundant throughout year	Cerrato (1986)
Mollusca			
Gastropoda			
Calyptraeidae			
Crepidula fornicata	ENSS	abundant	MSRC (1973)
Crepidula convexa	ENSS	abundant	MSRC (1973)
Muricidae			
Urosalpinx cinerea	ENMC	biomass-dominant	O'Connor (1972)
		abundant, Bellport Bay	WAPORA (1972)

Table 4 (continued)

Taxa	Function al Group	Distribution/ Abundance	Source
Nassariidae			
Nassarius obsoletus	ENMO	biomass-dominant	O'Connor (1972)
Bivalvia			
Cardiidae			
Laevicardium mortoni	INSS	dominant	MSRC (1973)
Mytilidae			
Mytilus edulis	ENSS	abundant	Cerrato (1986)
		biomass-dominant	O'Connor (1972)
		abundant	MSRC (1973)
		common food organism of GSB fishes	MSRC (1973)
Pectinidae			
Argopecten irradians	ENMS	not abundant in 1978	WAPORA (1982)
Solemyidae			
Solemya velum	INMDi	abundant	MSRC (1973)
Tellinidae			
Tellina agilis	INSDs	dominant	MSRC (1973)
Veneridae			
Gemma gemma	INSS	dominant in Brookhaven	WAPORA (1982)
		abundant	MSRC (1973)
Mercenaria mercenaria	INSS	biomass-dominant	O'Connor (1972)
		dominant	MSRC (1973)
Arthropoda			
Amphipoda (Order)			
Ampeliscidae			
Ampelisca abdita	ITSDs	dominant	Cerrato (1986)
Lysianassidae			
Lysianopsis alba	INMDs	abundant throughout year dominant	Cerrato (1986)
			MSRC (1973)
Phoxocephalidae			
Eobrolgus spinosus	INMDi	abundant	MSRC (1973)
Decapoda (Order)			
Cancridae			
Cancer irroratus	ENMO	present in Islip	WAPORA (1982)
Crangonidae			
Crangon septemspinosa	ENMO	north shore of Fire Island	Raposa & Oviatt (2000)

10

Table 4 (continued)

Taxa	Functional Group	Distribution/ Abundance	Source
Palaemonidae			
Palaemonetes pugio	ENMO	north shore of Fire Island	Raposa & Oviatt (2000)
Hippolytidae			
Hippolyte pleuracanthus	ENMO	north shore of Fire Island	Raposa & Oviatt (2000)
Portunidae			
Callinectes sapidus	ENMO	north shore of Fire Island	Raposa & Oviatt (2000)
Panopeidae			
Dyspanopeus sayi	ENMO	biomass-dominant abundant near Clam Pond abundant	O'Connor (1972) WAPORA (1982) MSRC (1973)
Panopeus herbstii	ENMO	abundant near Clam Pond	WAPORA (1982)
Isopoda (Order)			
Idoteidae			
Idotea balthica	ENMO	abundant	MSRC (1973)
Chordata			
Ascidiacea			
Styelidae			
Botryllus schlosseri	ENSS	biomass-dominant	O'Connor (1972)

Primary harvested finfishes

The finfish species most frequently landed by commercial harvesters from the FIIS region are bluefish, winter flounder, summer flounder, weakfish, Atlantic silversides, and menhaden (Bokuniewicz et al. 1993). The recreational species landed within GSB have not been described in detail since Briggs (1962), but total recreational landings for New York as a whole suggest that fluke, winter flounder, bluefish, weakfish, tautog, and black sea bass are the main species landed in the bay (Bokuniewicz et al. 1993).

Some of the fish species landed in the FIIS region are present only transiently as older juveniles and adults. Such species would include striped bass, menhaden, eels, and weakfish. These species do not use GSB as a spawning and nursery area. The ecological value of FIIS waters to these species is probably a direct function of the proportional shoreline length that FIIS represents in relation to the overall coastline. Other species use FIIS waters as both nursery grounds for young-of-the-year (YOY) stages as well as adults. For these species, the value of FIIS habitat may greatly exceed its proportional contribution to the coastline, and thereby be of greater importance. The ecology and habitat requirements of species using FIIS waters as both juvenile nursery and adult feeding areas is described below.

Bluefish (*Pomatomus saltatrix*) -- Both YOY and adult bluefish are of great ecological importance in GSB and are abundant on both the Atlantic Ocean and bay shores of FIIS during the late spring, summer and fall. They represent one of the most abundant piscivores in the system. Bluefish spawn over the continental shelf in spring and summer. The recruitment of YOY bluefish migrating into GSB has been studied in great detail (see citations in Bokuniewicz et al. 1993). The arrival in GSB of YOY bluefish from continental shelf waters occurs in two periods: a May and June recruitment consisting of spring-spawned fish, and an August recruitment of summer-spawned fish. Young bluefish in GSB are found in the shore zone where they feed largely on young silversides in June and July, and then shift their diet to young bay anchovy in August and September (Juanes 1992). Adult bluefish congregate near the inlets and channels and feed on a variety of species including sand lance, menhaden, bay anchovy, butterfish, and squid.

Winter flounder *(Pseudopleuronectes americanus)* -- Winter flounder are probably resident in GSB and adjacent Atlantic waters most of the year, and may represent a subpopulation unique to the area. Spawning occurs in GSB from about March to May and, together with sand lance, winter flounder are a major portion of the winter ichthyoplankton (Bokuniewicz et al. 1993). Juveniles and adults are generally found on muddy bottoms of bays, coves and tidal creeks. Although winter flounder are generally believed to migrate offshore as temperatures increase in summer, Olla et al. (1969) showed that some winter flounder remain in GSB throughout the summer, burying themselves in the sediment when temperatures exceed 23° C. Winter flounder feed primarily on a variety of benthic invertebrates including amphipods, polychaetes, *Crangon septemspinosa*, *Mya arenaria*, and *Mytilus edulis*. The larvae feed mainly on copepods. Winter flounder in GSB are themselves preyed upon by a variety of species, including striped bass, summer flounder and bluefish.

Summer flounder or fluke (*Paralichthys dentatus*) -- Summer flounder spawn over the continental shelf in the fall. Young fish enter estuaries along the mid-Atlantic coast in the winter and spring (Able et al. 1989). Poole (1961) found that young summer flounder in GSB grow rapidly during their first summer, reaching a size of about 23 cm by autumn. Adult summer flounder migrate into GSB in May. Summer flounder feed mainly on crustaceans and fish. Poole (1964) found that sand shrimp (*Crangon*), winter flounder, and blue crabs constituted 28.5%, 27.8% and 12.1%, respectively, of the total weight of food contents of summer flounder in GSB.

Reef species: tautog (*Tautoga onitis*) and black sea bass (*Centropristis striata*) -- The biology of tautog has been studied extensively in Fire Island Inlet (see citations in Bokuniewicz et al. 1993). Spawning occurs in the summer and newly-settled juveniles occupy shallow, vegetated (eelgrass or *Ulva)* habitats beginning in late summer, where they remain until reaching a size where they can take up residence on reef structures. Shallow water vegetated habitat coupled with deep water reefs are critical habitat requirements for these species. Fish tend to be active by day and inactive by night. Older fish move offshore in winter, but younger fish remain on inshore reefs, enduring the winter in a state of torpor. Young tautog in eelgrass beds feed primarily on copepods and amphipods in GSB. Larger tautog in GSB feed primarily on the mussel, *Mytilus edulis,* in May and June (Olla et al. 1975).

Forage finfish species and their habitats

Several finfish species common in FIIS waters are a relatively minor component of area fisheries but play a critical ecological role in the trophic system of GSB, serving as forage for many resource species and transferring energy from lower to higher levels of the food web.

Atlantic silverside (*Menidia menidia*) --The dominant member of the ichthyofauna of GSB throughout much of the year is *M. menidia*. Hanlon (1983) found that 79% of the fish captured by all methods (trawls, beach seines, gill nets) in his survey were *M. menidia*. Raposa and Oviatt's (2000) study of Fire Island National Seashore also showed that *Menidia* numerically dominates among fishes captured close to shore.

Habitats utilized by silversides vary with life stage. In the spring, spawning occurs *en masse* amongst schools of fish that deposit eggs at specific locations where large mats of intertidal algae are found. Intertidal spawning protects the embryos from aquatic predators. In the summer and fall, larvae and young juveniles are found in the neuston close to shore over both vegetated and unvegetated intertidal and subtidal bottoms. They are extremely abundant in the shore zone virtually everywhere in the bay. Shallow inshore waters such as GSB are the prime habitat of silversides. They are found in offshore waters of the continental shelf only in mid-winter when water temperatures close to shore drop to lethal levels (Conover and Murawski, 1982).

Silversides are primarily zooplanktivores. Grover (1982) reported that Atlantic silversides in GSB fed primarily on copepods during all seasons of the year. In the spring and early summer, however, up to 40% of the diet consisted of fish eggs and larvae. The silverside is an important forage species for piscivorous fishes. Juanes (1992) reported that *M. menidia* is a major portion of the diet of young-of-the-year (YOY) bluefish in GSB. In addition, the Atlantic silverside is consumed by several other piscivores in the bay including striped bass (Schaefer 1970; Briggs and O'Connor 1971), weakfish, and summer flounder (Poole 1964).

M. menidia is also a commercially harvested species as it represents one of the main species used as bait in the recreational fishery. Commercial landings of silversides of about 50,000 lbs/yr have been harvested from Long Island's south shore for decades, with peak landings in excess of 200,000 lbs in the 1950s and 60s. Much of these landings probably come from GSB, possibly including the waters of FIIS.

Bay anchovy (*Anchoa mitchilli*)--The bay anchovy is also one of the major forage species found in GSB. Although its numerical abundance in beach seine samples is moderate (Hanlon 1983; Raposa and Oviatt 2000), its dominance in the summer ichthyoplankton suggests it is the dominant component of the water column fauna in the middle bay (Monteleone 1992). Castro and Cowen (1991) found that the peak in spawning of bay anchovy in GSB was in late June and July, and coincided with the summer peak in microzooplankton abundance. They found no difference between eelgrass and unvegetated areas of GSB in egg or larval densities (but see Shima and Cowen 1989), larval growth rates, or egg and yolk-sac larvae mortality rates of bay anchovy. Mortality of older bay anchovy larvae was higher over eelgrass beds than over unvegetated bottom, perhaps because of greater exposure to predators inhabiting the eelgrass beds. Bay anchovies are not, however, an estuarine-dependent species. They are also abundant in the open water column of continental shelf waters throughout most seasons of the year.

The bay anchovy is a major food source for piscivorous fishes in GSB. They constitute a large fraction of the diet of young bluefish in the bay during late summer and fall (Juanes 1992) and are also consumed by virtually every piscivore in the bay including striped bass (Schaefer 1970), summer flounder (Poole 1964), and weakfish (Merriner 1975).

Killifishes (*Fundulus heteroclitus*, mummichog; *Fundulus majalis*, striped killifish; *Cyprinodon variegatus*, sheepshead minnow)--Members of the family Cyprinodontidae are generally very abundant in the shore zone of FIIS. The mummichog predominates in high and low salt marsh habitats, especially salt marsh creeks, ditches, rivulets, or beaches where the sediment is soft, and/or where vegetation is present. The striped killifish prefers sandy bottom habitats. These differences in habitat preference are evident in Briggs and O'Connor's (1971) study in GSB. Hanlon (1983) generally collected about twice as many striped killifish as mummichog. The habitat types where he found mummichogs to outnumber striped killifish were over subtidal mud and gravel. *C. variegatus* may be found in either habitat, but both Briggs and O'Connor (1971) and Hanlon (1983) collected more over sandy bottoms than over naturally vegetated or mud habitats.

Killifishes feed on a variety of invertebrate marsh organisms including insect larvae (Kneib 1986). Because they rarely stray further than a few meters from the shoreline, they are not usually a large component of the diet of piscivorous fishes. On the other hand, they represent a major food source for crabs and wading birds (Kneib 1986). *F. heteroclitus* is used extensively as bait in the summer flounder fishery (Briggs and O'Connor 1971).

Fourspine stickleback (*Apeltes quadracus*)--The fourspine stickleback was the second- most abundant fish overall in Briggs and O'Connor's (1971) study of shore zone fishes, and it ranked first in abundance in naturally vegetated habitats. In Hanlon's (1983) study, however, the relative abundance of four-spine stickleback was less (overall rank=6) than found by Briggs and O'Connor (1971). Raposa and Oviatt (2000) also found *Apeltes* to be an abundant species in vegetated and marsh habitat along the FIIS/GSB shoreline. The abundance of *Apeltes* was positively correlated with macroalgal but not eelgrass biomass. Sticklebacks spawn in the spring and summer and are nest-building species that use vegetation for nest concealment and protection from predators. *Apeltes* appears to remain in GSB throughout much of the year.

Due probably to their close association with cover and their armor of lateral plates and spines, sticklebacks do not represent a major fraction of the diet of most piscivores, but they have been found occasionally in the stomachs of striped bass (Schaefer 1970) and summer flounder (Briggs and O'Connor 1971).

Northern pipefish (*Syngnathus fuscus*)--Pipefish are abundant both as larvae in the summer plankton (Miller 1977) and as juveniles and adults in vegetated areas (Briggs and O'Connor 1971; Hanlon 1983). Raposa and Oviatt (2000) reported that the abundance of pipefish was positively correlated with eelgrass biomass within FIIS, and their adult morphology mimics that of eelgrass. They feed on zooplankton in the water column and are themselves consumed by summer flounder and striped bass. Pipefish represent a substantial fraction (~10%) of the diet of summer flounder in GSB (Poole 1964).

American sand lance (*Ammodytes americanus*) --A major component of the winter fish assemblage in GSB is probably the sand lance. Although this species does not appear to be abundant in GSB based on catches reported by Hanlon (1983), Briggs and O'Connor (1971), or other studies of GSB, this might be largely because of lack of sampling with appropriate gear in winter. Miller (1977) found that the sand lance was overall the most numerous larval fish collected in GSB. Larvae were collected from January to May with a peak production in late January through the end of February. Sand lance are likely to be abundant on both the Atlantic and GSB shores of FIIS.

American sand lance are found almost exclusively over sandy bottoms and are one of the most abundant fishes over the inner half of the continental shelf (Grosslein and Azarovitz 1982). They have the unique habit of burrowing in the sand in dense aggregations. They feed at all levels in the water column, primarily on copepods, crustacean larvae, chaetognaths, and various invertebrate and fish eggs (Grover 1982; Grosslein and Azarovitz 1982). The sand lance is itself preyed upon by numerous piscivores. In FIIS, the main predators on sand lance are likely to be adult bluefish, striped bass, weakfish, summer flounder, and birds.

Fish Habitat Utilization in FIIS

The major sources of information on the distribution and abundance of fishes by habitat in the FIIS and GSB are Briggs and O'Connor (1971) on shore zone fishes from naturally vegetated vs. sand-filled areas and Hanlon (1983), who provides extensive tables on the combined catches from otter trawls and beach seines in GSB, Moriches Bay and Shinnecock for nine different types of habitats. Raposa and Oviatt (2000) provide data for nekton collected with a small beach seine and throw traps from the north shore of Fire Island during May to October 1995. Schaefer (1967) characterized the fish fauna of the ocean beach side of FIIS. The summary provided below is based on a more detailed synthesis of available literature in Bokuniewicz et al. (1993).

Intertidal beach -- Intertidal beaches are used by several species as a spawning site. The Atlantic silverside deposits its eggs in filamentous algae (*Enteromorpha* sp.) or other vegetative material in the upper intertidal zone of salt marshes and open beaches where they are protected from predation by aquatic predators. The mummichog (*Fundulus heteroclitus*) also deposits eggs in the upper intertidal zone either on stems of *Spartina,* within empty mussel shells or amongst filamentous algae (Taylor and DiMichele, 1983). Both of these species spawn on a semi-lunar schedule that corresponds with the occurrence of new and full moons.

Salt marsh -- The primary inhabitants of polyhaline mid-Atlantic salt marshes are *M. menidia* and *Fundulus* spp. (Roundtree and Able, 1992). *C. variegatus* and *A. mitchilli* are also abundant but less so than the above species. Hanlon (1983) collected primarily striped killifish, Atlantic silversides, mummichogs, and bluefish (in descending order of abundance) from the salt marsh habitats of Long Island south shore bays he sampled.

Eelgrass beds -- Based on the work of Briggs and O'Connor (1971) in GSB, Hanlon (1983) in GSB, Moriches and Shinnecock Bays, and Raposa and Oviatt (2000), those species in GSB that are probably most dependent on eelgrass or other vegetated habitats include *A. quadracus, G. aculeatus, S. fuscus,* and juvenile *T. onitis* and *T. adspersus.* Other major species frequently captured over eelgrass beds but also caught frequently elsewhere include *M. menidia, F. heteroclitus, P. americanus,* and *C. variegatus.*

Non-vegetated shoals -- Unvegetated bay bottom is preferred habitat of several benthic fishes. Briggs and O'Connor (1971) found six species in GSB that were more abundant over sand-filled than vegetated habitats, the main ones being *M. menidia, F. majalis,* and *C. variegatus.* Hanlon (1983) caught relatively more *P. americanus* and P. *dentatus* in unvegetated than vegetated bottom habitats.

Water column -- The main species dependent on the water column are silversides, herrings and anchovies, and their predators, but this habitat is the least well-studied region of the bay, with little if any studies published to date. Bay anchovy is probably the dominant planktivore in the middle of the bay during much of the year, but the existence of a modest commercial fishery for menhaden suggests that they too may be an important component of the pelagic fauna. Atlantic silversides, which dominate virtually all habitats in GSB, are probably also very important in the water column especially close to shore. Both juvenile and adult bluefish are probably highly dependent on the abundance of silversides and anchovies in the pelagic zone, based on the dominance of these species in the diet.

16

Species of special concern

Protected marine species that are or might possibly be found within FIIS are noted in Table 5. This list excludes marine birds, which are outside the immediate scope of this report. The appearance of most of these protected species within the boundaries of FIIS is likely to be rare and ephemeral. The large whales are oceanic; any whale found in the very nearshore waters of the Atlantic Ocean within the Park will almost surely be disoriented and/or diseased or injured. Long Island's coastal waters are an important summer foraging area for (primarily) juvenile sea turtles. Of the several species of sea turtles reported from New York's waters, the Kemp's ridley (*Lepidochelys kempii*), green (*Chelonia mydas*) and leatherback (*Dermochelys coriacea*) are the most common. These animals are most frequently found in nearshore Atlantic Ocean waters off eastern Long Island, the Peconic-Gardiner's Bays System, and eastern Long Island Sound. Their occurrence within the waters of FIIS is infrequent.

Several seal species including harbor (*Phoca vitulina*), harp (*Pagophilus groenlandicus*), gray (*Halichoerus grypus*) have been found stranded on beaches within Great South Bay (e.g., Smith Point Park) and FIIS indicating that they are visitors to the area. Hooded seal (*Cystophora cristata*) have also been stranded along the Atlantic beaches of Long Island (e.g., East Hampton) (Riverside Foundation for Marine research and Preservation).

Beyond their infrequent and episodic occurrence within FIIS' marine waters, whales and sea turtles are highly migratory animals. Management measures implemented on their behalf through the FIIS General Management Plan are unlikely to have an impact on the status of whale or sea turtle populations. However, given their legally-protected status and the considerable public interest in their conservation, when a sea turtle or, especially, a whale is detected within the Park's marine waters, it is important that Park staff be familiar with federal laws and protocols governing public interactions with these animals.

While the northern diamondback terrapin (*Malaclemys t. terrapin*), or salt marsh turtle, is not an officially "listed" species in New York, there is widespread concern about the species' status on Long Island. This inhabitant of shallow coastal embayments along the U.S. East Coast is present in the Great South Bay, including areas within FIIS. *M.t. terrapin* nests in sandy areas adjacent to shallow estuarine embayments (Burger and Montevecchi, 1975). In recent years, nest predation by raccoons, foxes, and domestic dogs has resulted in low and variable diamondback terrapin nesting success in certain historically productive areas of Long Island, including Jamaica Bay and Oyster Bay on the Island's north shore. Of equal or perhaps greater concern is the potential impact of the burgeoning blue crab trap fishery in Great South Bay on these terrapins. Terrapins that enter baited crab traps often drown before the trap can be "tended" and the animals released. In 1990, New York State promulgated special regulations to limit direct harvests of diamondback terrapins, but these have no effect on the incidental take of terrapins in crab traps. It is recommended that studies be conducted to assess the scope and potential severity of threats to the diamondback terrapin within FIIS and the types of management approach most likely to successfully address these threats.

Table 5. Marine Protected Species within FIIS. E=endangered; T=threatened; SC=special concern; SR=special regulations. * Note all marine mammals are protected under the Marine Mammal Protection Act of 1972.

Species	Federal	NYS
Reptiles		
Sea turtle, green (*Chelonia mydas*)	T	T
Sea turtle, hawksbill (*Eretmochelys imbricata*)	E	E
Sea turtle, Kemp's ridley (*Lepidochelys kempii*)	E	E
Sea turtle,leatherback (*Dermochelys coriacea*)	E	E
Sea turtle, loggerhead (*Caretta caretta*)	T	T
Mammals*		
Whale, northern right (*Balaena glacialis*)	E	E
Whale, humpback (*Megaptera novaeanglia*)	E	E
Whale, blue (*Balaenoptera musculus*)	E	E
Whale, finback (*Balaenoptera physalus*)	E	E
Whale, sei (*Balaenoptera borealis*)	E	E
Whale, sperm (*Physeter catodon*)	E	E
Porpoise, harbor (*Phocoena phocoena*)	-	SC
Seal, harp (*Pagophilus groenlandicus*)	-	-
Seal, harbor (*Phoca vitulina*)	-	SR
Seal, gray (*Halichoerus grypus*)	-	-

DESCRIPTION OF FISHERIES OCCURRING IN THE FIIS REGION

Shellfisheries

Shellfish of potential recreational or commercial value found within FIIS boundaries include surfclam (*Spisula solidissima*), hard clam (*Mercenaria mercenaria*), blue mussel (*Mytilus edulis*), soft clam (*Mya arenaria*), oyster (*Crassostrea virginica*), bay scallop (*Argopecten irradians*), razor clam (*Ensis directus*), conch (*Busycotypus canaliculatum*), blue crab (*Callinectes sapidus*), Jonah crab (*Cancer borealis*), rock crab (*Cancer irroratus*), lady crab (*Ovalipes ocellatus*), spider crab (*Libinia dubia)* and (*L. emarginata*), and horseshoe crab (*Limulus polyphemus*). Commercial landings data for these species can generally be disaggregated down to the harvest from GSB as a whole, but not that portion of the bay within the FIIS region. Shellfish recreational catch and/or harvest effort data are not routinely collected within New York's Marine District and no quantitative estimates are available for these harvests. Other than the fishery for surfclams, which is an ocean fishery managed by New York State, shellfisheries conducted within GSB are managed primarily by the three towns bordering the bay: Babylon, Islip, and Brookhaven. The towns issue annual commercial shellfishing permits to town residents; Babylon and Islip also issue non-commercial (recreational/personal) shellfishing permits. Reciprocity agreements for commercial shellfish permits exist between adjacent towns. Commercial shellfish harvesters within GSB must also possess a state shellfish diggers permit issued by the NYS Department of Environmental Conservation. Figures 1-6 show commercial harvests of various shellfish from Great South Bay, with the exception of surf clams, which are harvested from the nearshore waters of the Atlantic Ocean.

Surfclam - - A commercial dredge fishery for surfclams (*Spisula solidissima*) has existed in the state waters (0-3 miles) south of Fire Island for over 50 years. In 2005, twenty-two vessels were licensed to participate in this limited entry fishery. The primary harvesting area is west of Fire Island Inlet and outside the FIIS boundary. The inshore region (0-1 mile) between Fire Island Inlet and Moriches Inlet, however, occasionally has a large surfclam set. For example, in 2002 this region contained 26% of the surfclam biomass along the south shore of Long Island (NYS DEC 2002). Because of their deep draft, surfclam vessels do not harvest regularly within shallow waters. The NYS Department of Environmental Conservation manages this state fishery through an annual harvest quota and daily/weekly per vessel catch limits. In 2005, the annual harvest quota for surfclams along the south shore of Long Island was 500,000 bushels (Maureen Davidson, NYSDEC, pers. comm., 2005).

Hard clam - - The hard clam (*Mercenaria mercenaria* L.) is an important economic and commercial species that has declined significantly in GSB. In 2003, commercial landings from the bay were 7,398 bushels, almost one hundred times lower than the peak landings of 700,000 bushels reported in 1976 (Figure 1). The abundance of hard clams in Great South Bay rose dramatically beginning in the mid-1960's because of a succession of excellent sets (COSMA, 1985). The distribution and abundance of hard clams in GSB is known primarily from periodic surveys by the Towns of Babylon, Islip (e.g., Buckner 1984), and Brookhaven (e.g., Kassner et al. 1991) and from an extensive study by WAPORA Inc (1982). Little is known of the historic abundance and distribution of hard clams on the bottomlands formerly owned by the Blue Points Company and now under the control of The Nature Conservancy. Moriches Bay has never supported a highly productive hard clam fishery, and the distribution of hard clams in this bay has not been documented.

The hard clam population of GSB collapsed over the past 30 years and current hard clam densities throughout much of the bay are less than 1 sq. m. The towns issued fewer than 100 commercial diggers permits in 2003 and, likely, very few of these permitees used their permits (J. Kassner, Town of Brookhaven, pers. communication, 2004). It is speculated that the recreational catch of hard clams in GSB may now exceed the commercial harvest. The dire condition of the hard clam fishery in GSB has prompted intense interest in developing a bay-wide plan to restore the hard clam to something akin to its former abundance. Development of this plan is being headed by the Bluepoints Bottomlands Council, a group organized under the aegis of The Nature Conservancy and including representation from the state, the towns, NPS/FIIS, Suffolk County, baymen's groups, local universities, and environmental NGO's.

Landings of other commercial mollusk species are given in Figures 2-6. All of these species support only minor and episodic commercial activity.

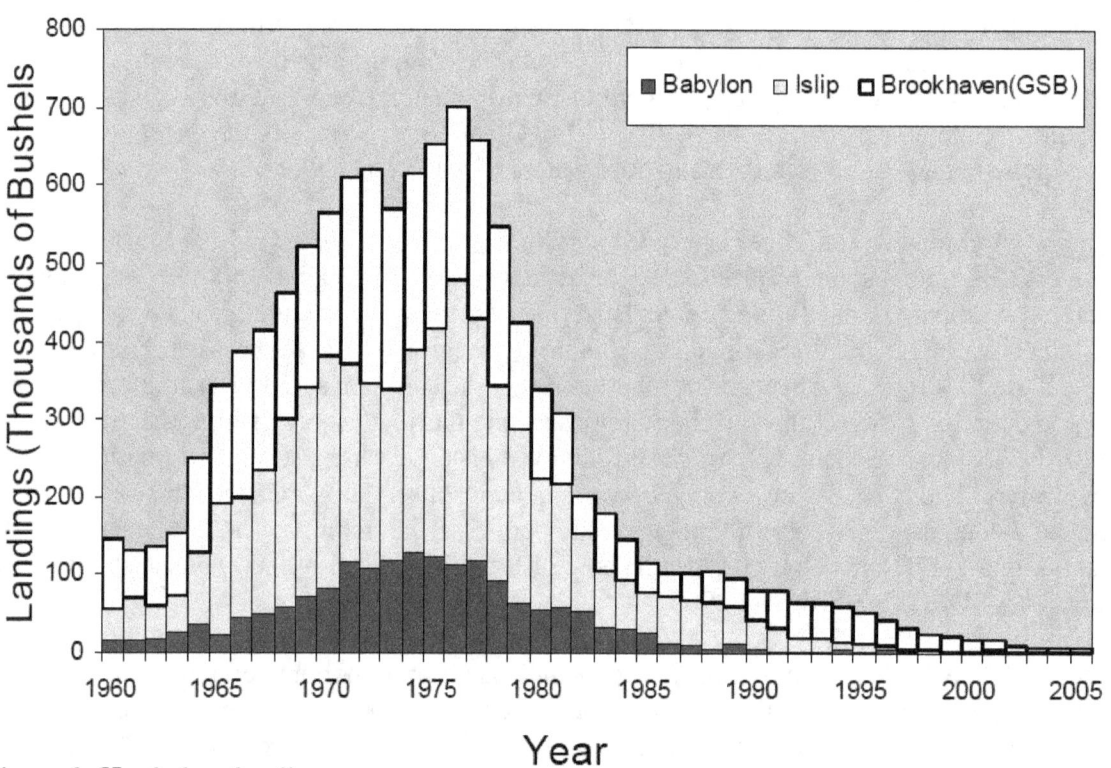

Figure 1. Hard clam landings.

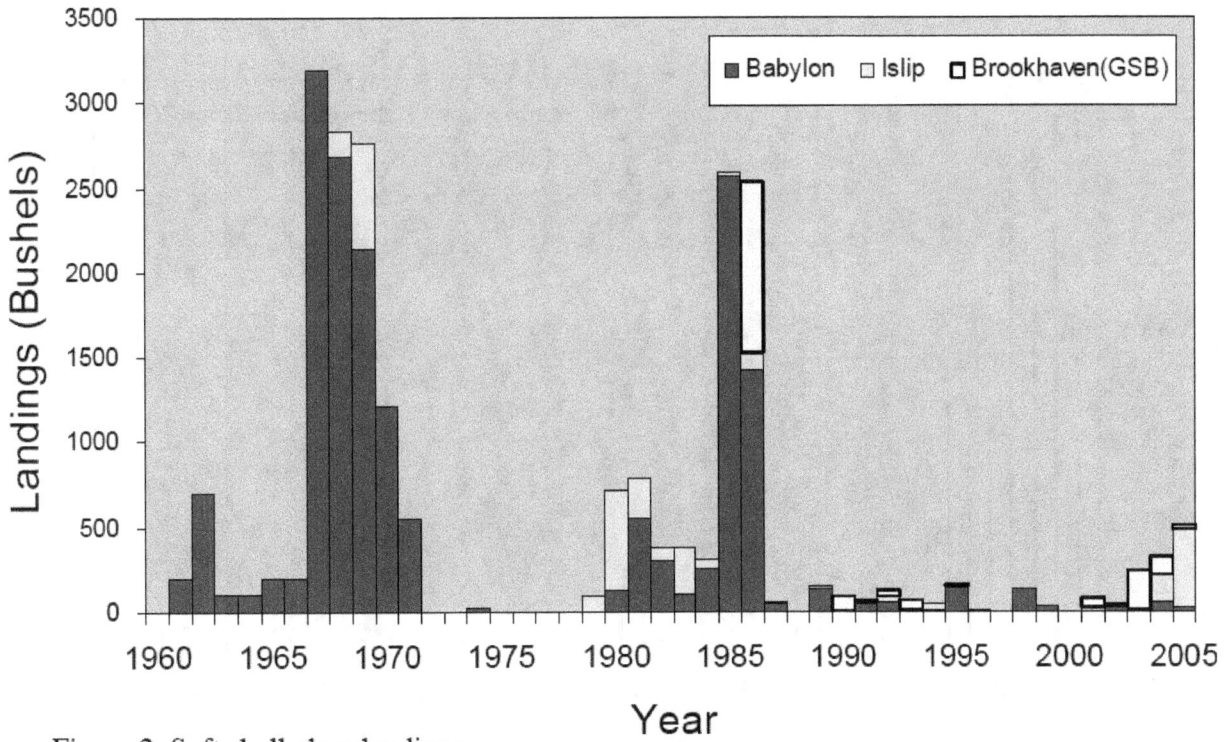

Figure 2. Soft shell clam landings.

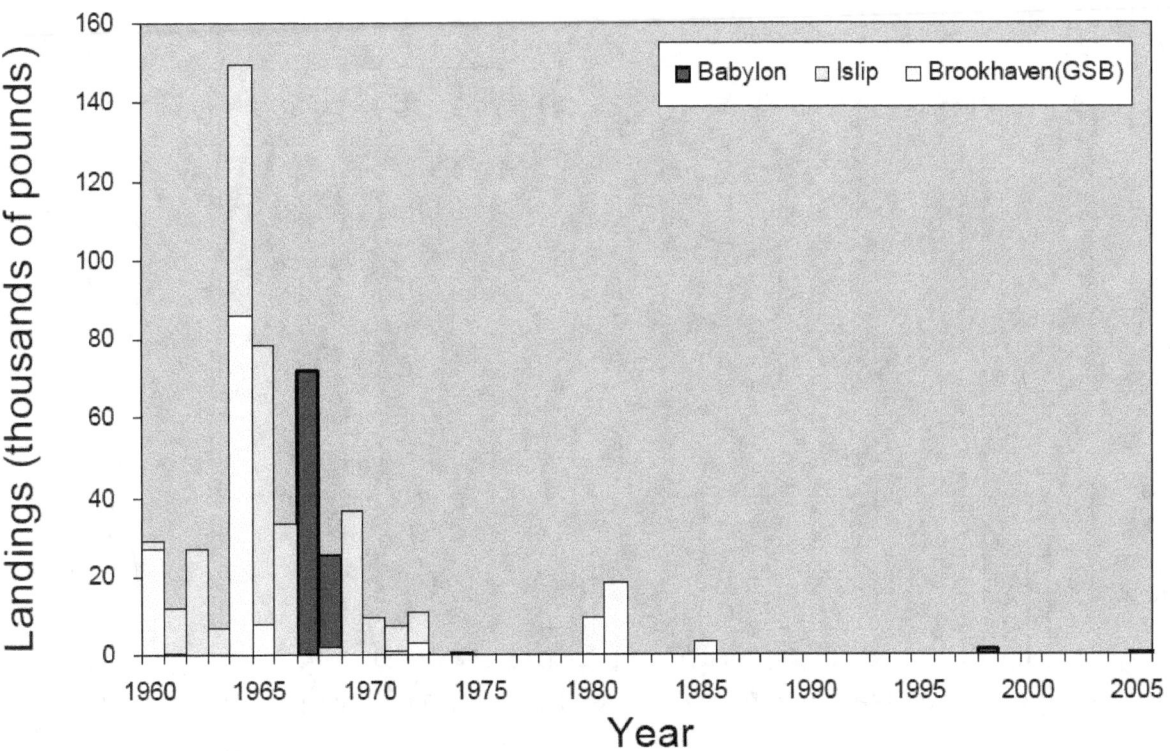

Figure 3. Bay scallop landings.

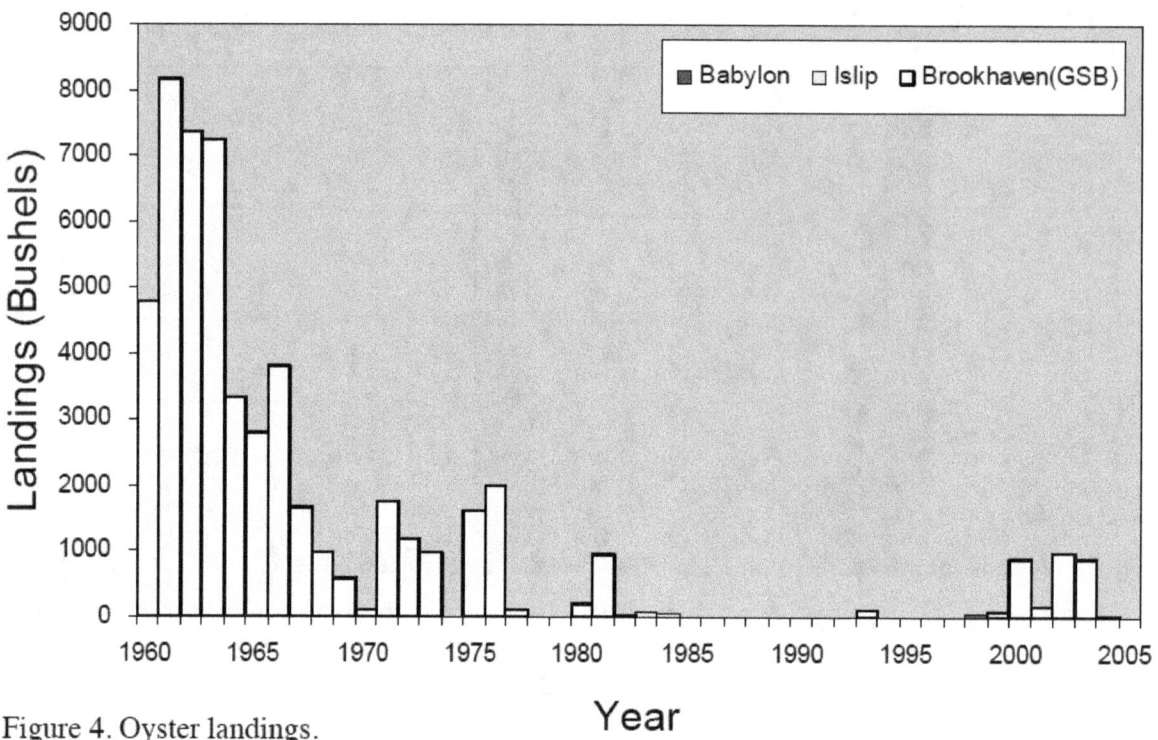

Figure 4. Oyster landings.

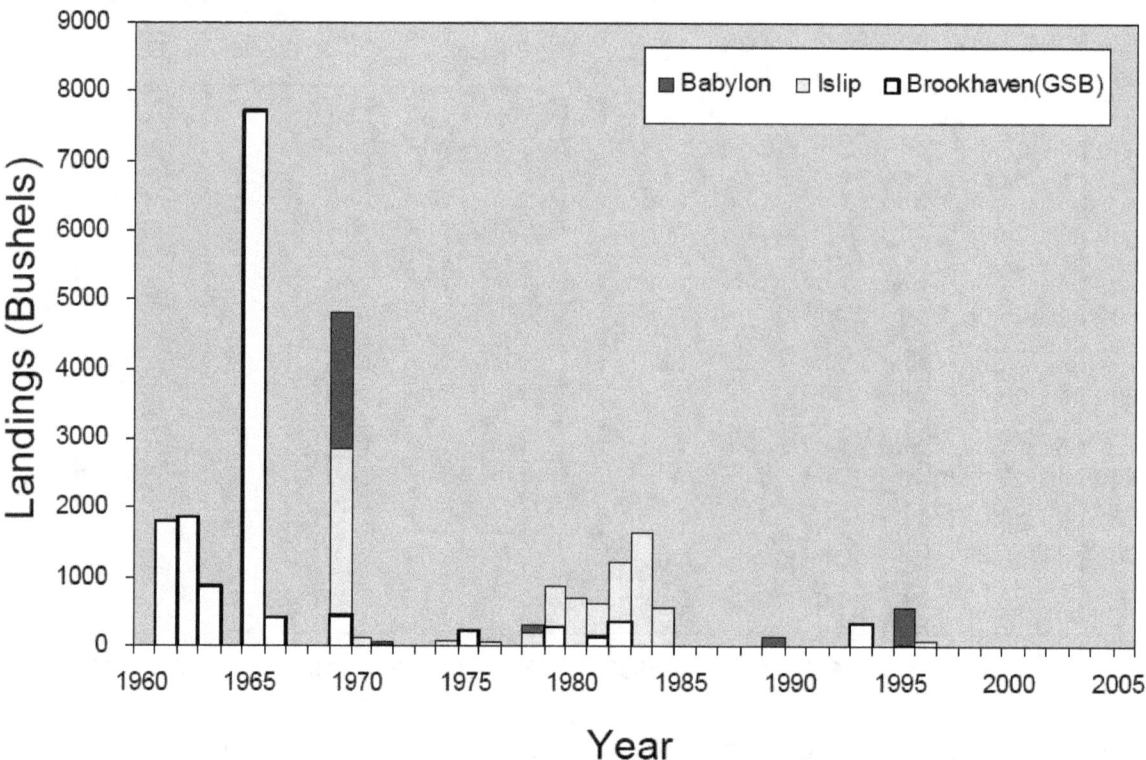

Figure 5. Mussel landings.

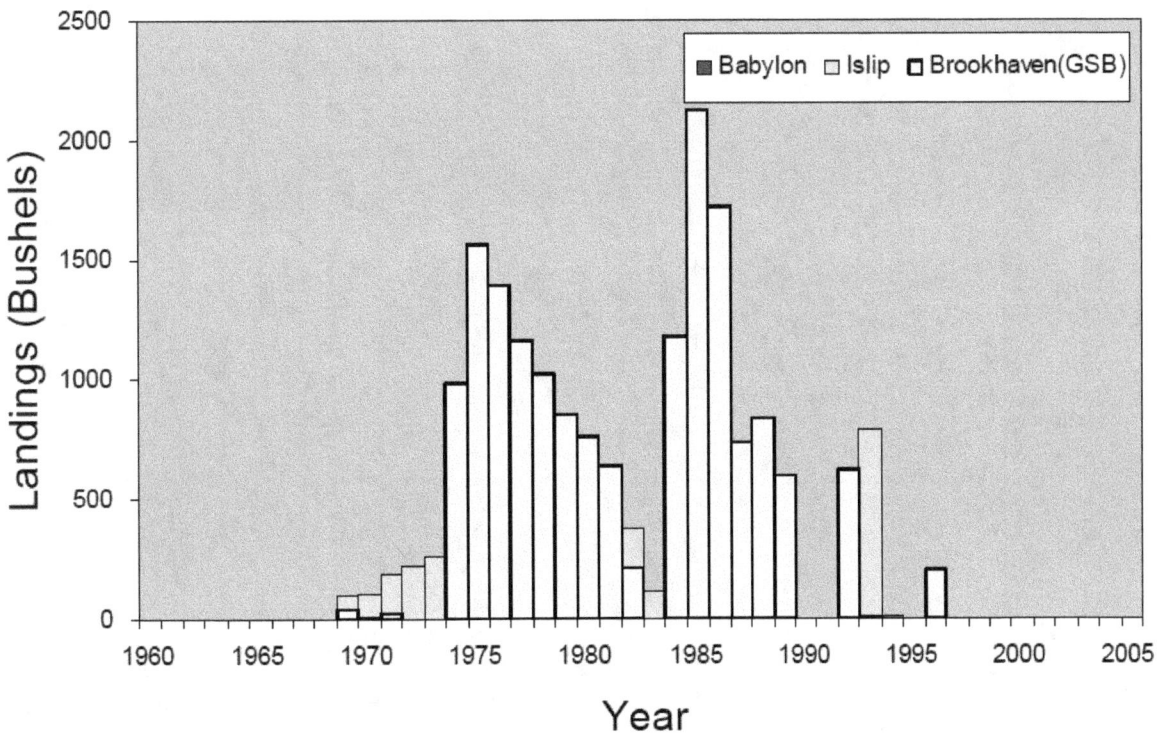

Figure 6. Conch landings.

Blue crab - - Commercial landings of blue crabs in New York State increased significantly from the mid-1970s to the mid-1990s (SSER 1999) (Figure 7). Permit survey data reported in SSER (1999) suggests that the south shore bays produce considerably more blue crabs than any other New York State area (Table 6). Blue crabs are commercially harvested by pots during the warm months and dredges in winter. Recreational harvesting by collapsible traps, hand lines, and dip nets also takes place (SSER 1999), but the level of recreational crabbing activity in the FIIS region is unknown.

Other crabs - - Minor fisheries exist in GSB for Jonah crabs (Figure 8), rock crabs (Figure 9), lady crabs, and spider crabs. The latter species is used only for bait. Both rock and lady crabs are part of the high salinity (> 28) assemblage closely associated with the inlets (WAPORA Inc 1982, SSER 1999). No distributional data are available for the other two species.

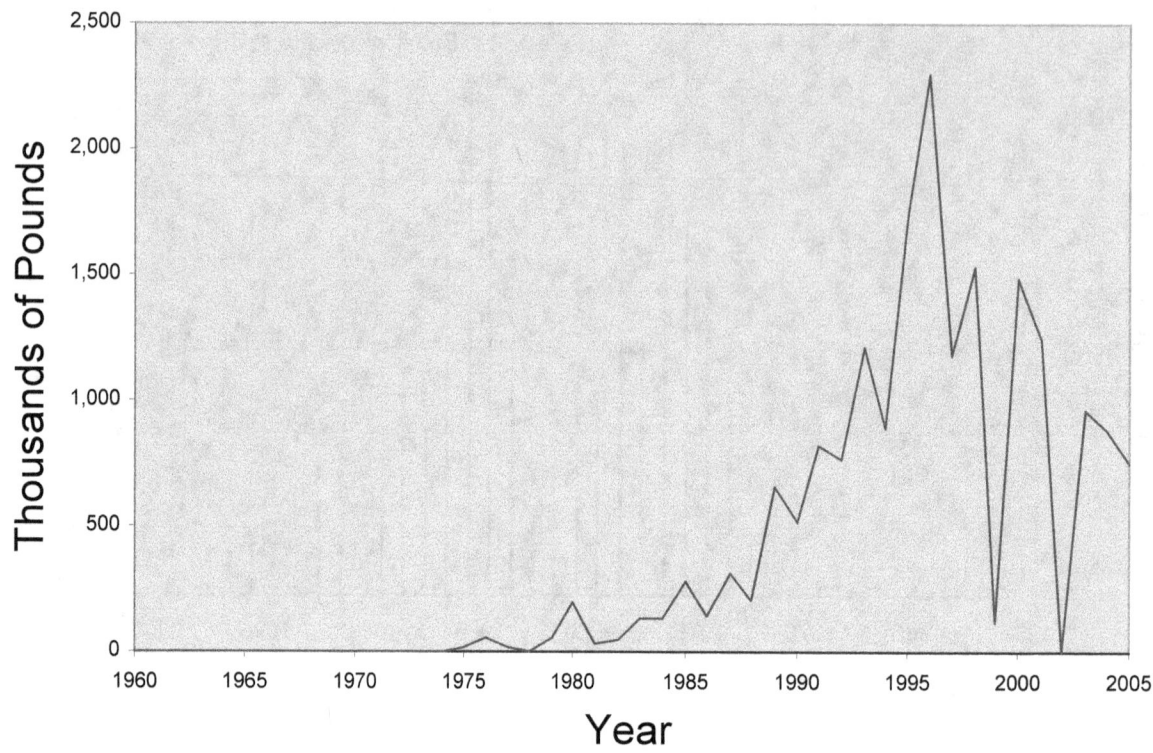

Figure 7. Blue crab landings- New York State.

Table 6. Regional distribution of New York crab landings based on 1997 annual permit survey. Table modified from NY Department of State (SSER 1999). Data source: NY State Department of Environmental Conservation.

Crab Species	Ocean	Long Island Sound	South Shore Bays	East (Peconics& Block Island Sound)	West (New York Harbor, Hudson R., & NY Bight)
Blue	5%	1%	74%	2%	18%
Horseshoe	13%	3%	31%	52%	0%
Jonah Crab	63%	23%	13%	1%	0%
Green	0%	22%	70%	8%	0%
Rock	64%	8%	21%	4%	2%
Hermit	4%	64%	6%	27%	0%
Lady	65%	0%	26%	1%	7%
Fiddler	0%	0%	0%	100%	0%
Spider	8%	47%	0%	45%	0%

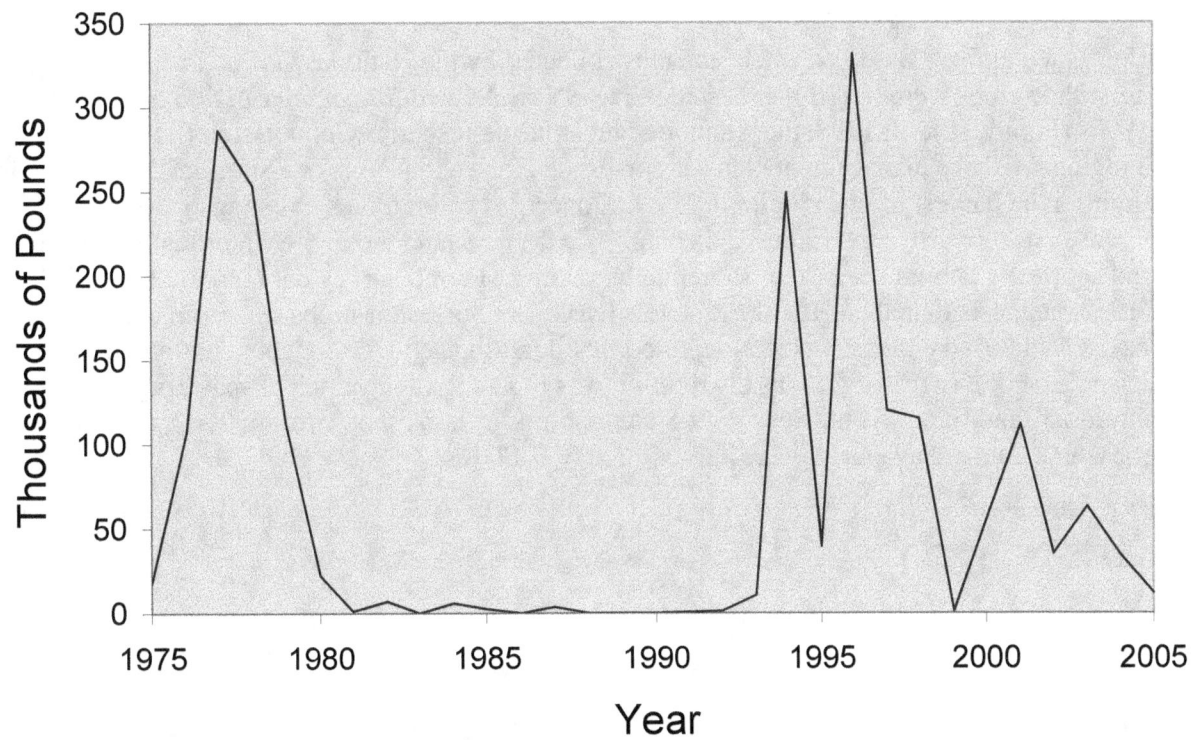

Figure 8. Jonah crab landings – New York State.

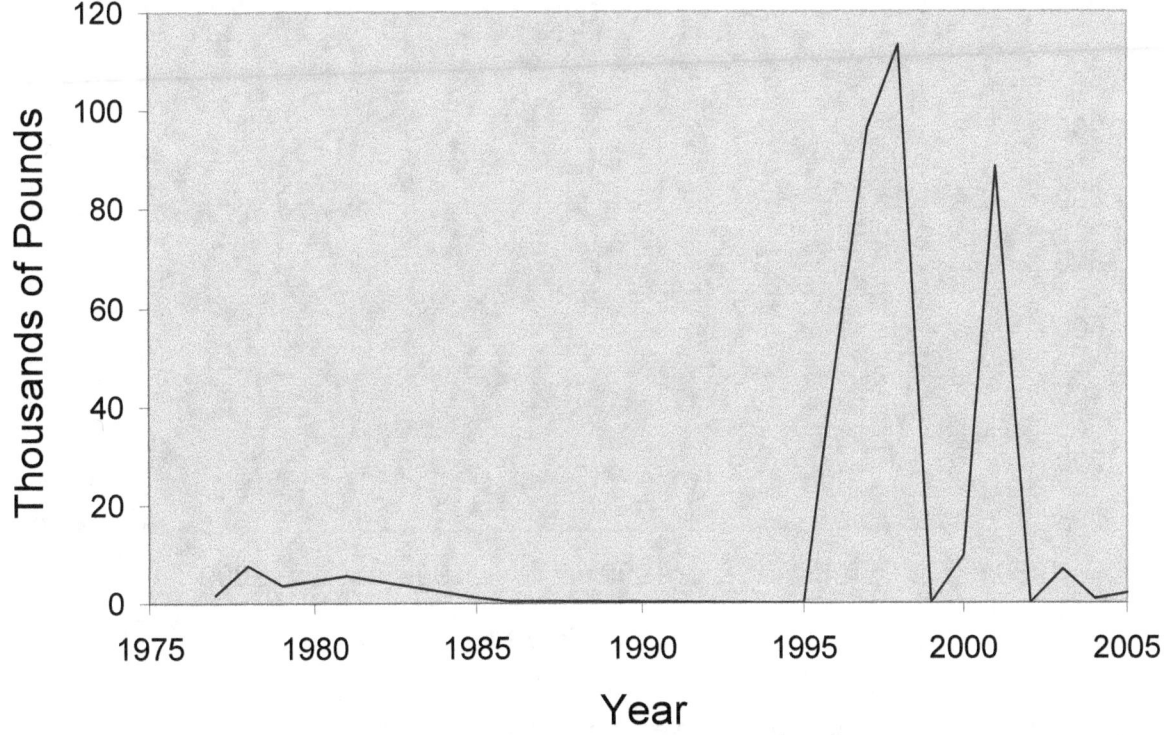

Figure 9. Rock crab landings – New York State.

Horseshoe crab - - Based on catch statistics collected by the National Marine Fisheries Service, horseshoe crabs were heavily harvested in New York State during a brief period in the mid-1990s (Figure 10). In 1998, the Atlantic States Marine Fisheries Commission (ASMFC) adopted a regional fishery management plan for horseshoe crabs and New York State adopted regulations limiting the harvest of this species in 1999. Concerns centered on harvesting of the species for use as bait, primarily in eel traps and conch (whelk) pots, and the loss of intertidal beach/sand flat spawning habitat because of shoreline hardening. Permit survey data reported in SSER (1999) suggests that about 1/3 of the state's harvest of horseshoe crabs was from the south shore bays (Table 6). WAPORA (1982) reported that horseshoe crabs were abundant only on the Fire Island side of eastern GSB. This distribution was linked to their principal spawning areas (i.e., intertidal sand flats). Total New York State landings of horseshoe crabs in 2002, the latest year for which data are available, were approximately 6000 lbs.

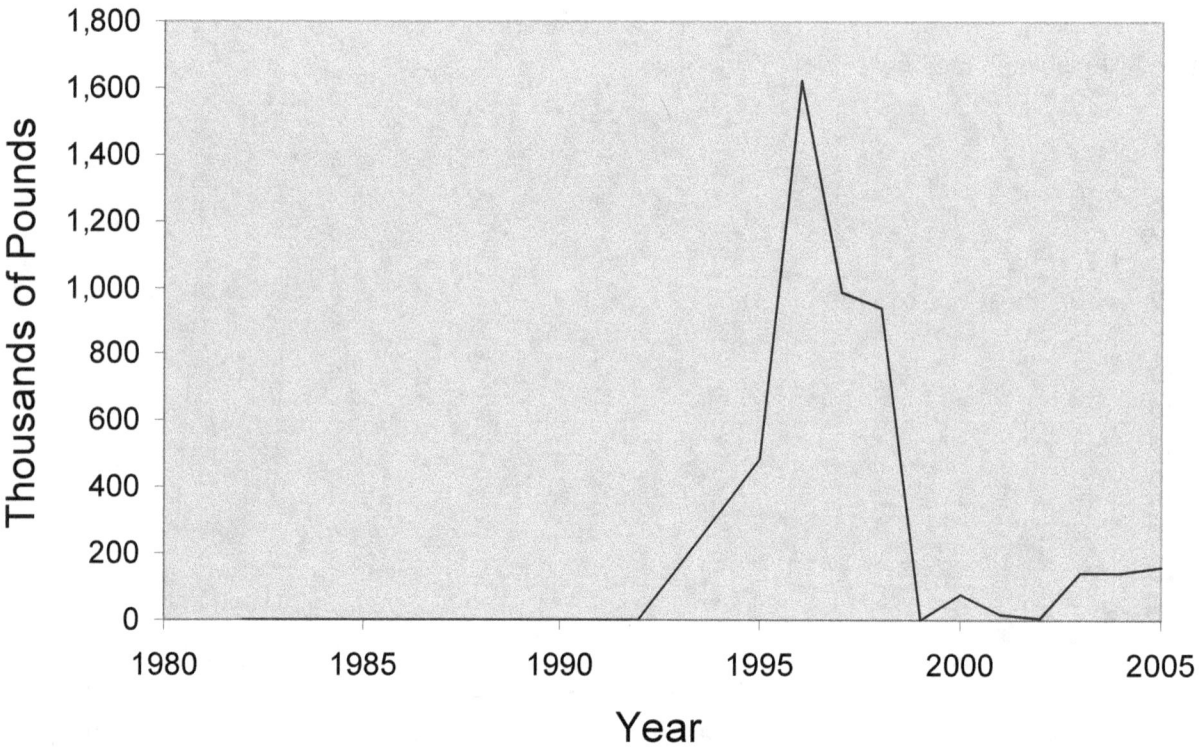

Figure 10. Horseshoe crab landings – New York State

Finfisheries

Commercial Finfisheries

Commercial harvests of finfish within FIIS boundaries are undocumented in Great South Bay. There is a small seasonal (spring/summer) gillnet fishery aimed primarily at menhaden (*Brevoortia tyrannus*) to supply bait for the lobster and crab pot fisheries as well as the recreational fisheries. Seine fisheries provide Atlantic silversides (*Menidia menidia*) and lesser amounts of several other forage species, again for use as bait. Eels (*Anguilla rostrata*) and, until recently oyster toadfish (*Opsanus tao*) are regularly harvested from bay waters with pots. The fishery for toadfish was of relatively brief duration and anecdotal evidence suggests that this species is now uncommon in GSB and rarely taken. Commercial trawling is prohibited anywhere within the bay.

Recreational Finfisheries

An active headboat (partyboat) fishery is located in the vicinity of Fire Island Inlet, near the western end of the Park. Boats from the boat basin at nearby Captree State Park fish in this location, as those from West Sayville, Orowoc Creek, and other maritime centers on the mainland. Target species include fluke, black sea bass, scup, blackfish and bluefish. The Captree headboat fleet alone includes more than 30 vessels that, in the 1990's, carried more than 300,000 passengers annually (Steadman 1999). While no documented numbers are available on the current number of headboats or their fares fishing the waters of FIIS, recent severe limits placed on recreational fisheries for some of the target species —lowered possession limits, increased minimum size limits, and shortened open seasons – are generally believed to have led to a decline in the activity of Long Island's charter and, especially, headboat fleet. Fishing from private boats also occurs in this same location, although there are no data describing the magnitude of this. Most of the bay waters within FIIS jurisdiction are very shallow and probably support little recreational fishing activity.

Limited opportunities exist for shore-based recreational angling along most of the Park's GSB shoreline and these are found primarily at Sailors Haven, Barrett beach, and Watch Hill. Intertidal marsh lines much of the bay shoreline of the Park, making access difficult for shore-based anglers. Conversely, recreational fishing is a frequent, albeit largely seasonal, activity along the ocean beaches of FIIS. The Park issues beach driving permits to fishermen wishing to fish the oceanfront beach in the Otis Pike High Dune Wilderness Area (Smith Point to Long Cove) for bluefish and/or striped bass. Sportsmen's Vehicular Permits are available for the period 15 September – 31 December each year. In 2003, the Seashore issued 140 such permits (NPS 2003).

LIVING MARINE RESOURCE AND RELATED HABITAT MANAGEMENT JURISDICTIONS & AUTHORITIES

Most of the living marine resources found within the administrative boundaries of FIIS are transboundary; i.e., they move across the unit's administrative boundaries as either adults and/or as planktonic larvae. What does not move into and out of the park are the habitats where these LMR's are found, although none of the habitats found in the Park are unique and similar habitats can be found outside the Park. However, for some habitat types (e.g., intertidal wetlands), the acreage found within FIIS is a large fraction of the total amount of this habitat in GSB. The LMR and LMR habitat-related policies and management measures implemented within FIIS need to be consistent with and complimentary to those of other agencies in the region who share jurisdiction with FIIS over living marine resources, their habitats, and human activities that influence both. Below is an abbreviated description of the respective jurisdictions and authorities of these agencies.

NPS/FIIS

The FIIS administrative boundaries encompass the tidal waters on both sides of Fire Island from the eastern end of Robert Moses State Park to Moriches Inlet and including Smith Point County Park on the eastern end of the island. The fringing marshes and marsh islands located on the northern side of Fire Island are within these boundaries, as are the tidal waters of Great South Bay to a point in the Bay generally 4,000 feet from mean high water. On the Atlantic Ocean, the FIIS boundary extends to a distance of 1,000 feet from mean high water.

The enabling legislation of the Seashore conveys to the Secretary of the Interior broad authority to "administer and protect the Fire Island National Seashore with the primary aim of conserving the natural resources located there." There is no regulation that specifically authorizes commercial finfish or shellfish harvesting within the Seashore, and thus such harvesting is currently prohibited and would require a special regulation to be allowed. Recreational harvests are consistent with NPS national regulations. It is noted that much of the bay and ocean bottom, or submerged areas, within the FIIS boundary are not owned by the federal government, but since fishing and shellfishing occurs throughout the water the regulations prohibiting commercial activities remain.

NYS Department of Environmental Conservation

The New York State Department of Environmental Conservation (DEC) is charged with protection, conservation, and management of living marine resources within the State's Marine District (all tidal areas south of the Tappan Zee Bridge), including finfish, shellfish, marine habitat protection, and marine water quality. Some of the LMR protections afforded by the state are found in law (Environmental Conservation Law) and some in regulations promulgated by DEC under authorities granted the agency by the New York State Legislature. The Bureau of Marine Resources is the cognizant unit for marine fisheries management within DEC's Division of Fish, Wildlife, and Marine Resources. Because the bulk of the State's living marine resources are migratory and/or multi-jurisdictional, DEC's living marine resource management programs often operate under state-federal management plans through the Atlantic States Marine Fisheries

Commission (ASMFC) or with the New England Fishery Management Council or Mid-Atlantic Fishery Management Council. The goal of these plans is to rebuild, retain and manage marine fishery stocks through direct fishery management measures (minimum size limits, net mesh regulations, for example) and through fishery habitat conservation and protection. DEC is also responsible for certification of shellfish growing areas and the oversight of the shellfish industry to ensure the public health and limit the incidence of shellfish-borne human diseases.

Suffolk County

Several agencies of Suffolk County conduct programs related to living marine resources and/or their habitats. The Department of Public Works manages County dredging projects in GSB and Moriches Bay as well as other waters. The Department of Parks and Recreational manages Smith Point County Park, which forms the easternmost portion of FIIS. The Department of Planning undertakes a variety of planning activities on land-use, water quality protection, and natural resource protection in marine waters adjacent to the County. The Suffolk County Department of Health Services monitors sewage treatment plants, several of which discharge into GSB. It has conducted ambient water quality monitoring in the bay for over 20 years. The Department of Health Services also conducts bathing beach bacterial monitoring on behalf of the NYS Department of Health, monitors and controls mosquito breeding in coastal marshes, and permits septic systems along the perimeter of GSB.

Babylon, Islip, and Brookhaven Towns

With the exception of 13,000 acres in the center of GSB owned by The Nature Conservancy (see below), the three towns of Babylon, Islip, and Brookhaven own the bottomlands of Great South Bay and Moriches Bay. Each town is responsible for managing the shellfish resources on their bottomlands. As noted, the towns issue permits to residents to harvest shellfish and have a variety of other shellfish-related management authorities under ordinances adopted by their town boards. The towns issue wetlands and waterways permits for activities occurring in or near a wetland or surface water.

The Nature Conservancy

The Nature Conservancy owns approximately 13,000 acres of bottomland in Great South Bay, the property formerly owned by The Bluepoints Oyster Company. Their ownership does not extend to the overlying waters and, thus, they have overlapping jurisdiction with NPS/FIIS in the southern part of their property, within 4,000 feet of the barrier island. The Conservancy established the Bluepoints Bottomlands Council to help it develop a long-term management plan for these underwater lands.

South Shore Estuary Reserve (SSER) Office

The SSER Office's primary responsibility is to facilitate implementation of the SSER Comprehensive Management Plan, developed by a council with membership drawn from local governments, NPS/FIIS, Nassau and Suffolk Counties and local towns and villages, in addition to non-profit organizations and interested individuals. The SSER area extends from Reynold's

Channel in Hempstead Bay east to the Shinnecock Canal. Chapter 3 of the Comprehensive Management Plan deals with protecting and restoring the living resources of the estuary, including shellfish fisheries, finfish fisheries, SAV, wetlands, and the protection and enhancement of ecosystem functioning. Other topical areas such as protection or improvement of water quality involves initiatives called watershed action plans, which attempt to get local land users to implement practices that will protect water quality in the estuary.

RECOMMENDATIONS: THE ROLE OF FIIS IN CONSERVATION OF MARINE RESOURCES

General goals and objectives

As stated in the FIIS 1998 strategic plan, one of the prime missions of the park is to preserve natural resources, including barrier island dynamics and ecology, biodiversity, and wilderness. At the same time, the Seashore is committed to providing access and recreational opportunities for visitors in a natural setting. The proximity of densely populated urban and suburban areas represents a difficult challenge, but also offers a great opportunity in achieving these stated goals.

In general, two different approaches to the management of the LMR's of FIIS could be considered. The first would be to treat FIIS as an oasis. Under the oasis model, management would concentrate solely on the LMR's and habitats found explicitly within the FIIS boundary, exercising control over human access and extraction activities to the full extent permitted by law, much like terrestrial preserves are managed. The second would be to recognize that due to the extensive larval dispersal patterns and adult migratory behavior of many marine species, marine ecosystems are inherently open-ended. FIIS is an integral part of an open network of habitats linking GSB to other south shore bays and the mid-Atlantic coastal ecosystems. It contains essential habitat for certain life stages of many important marine resources but it represents the sole habitat for virtually none, even at the level of an individual organism. Hence, unlike the terrestrial realm in the coastal Northeast, where individuals of many plants and animals and their offspring can be expected to live their entire life cycle within a park (perhaps except for avifauna and large mammals), most marine flora and fauna will cross the FIIS boundary at some point and spend much of their lifetime outside the park.

To protect park marine resources, it seems most appropriate to adopt a network model that emphasizes the role that park habitats play within the larger marine context. To do so successfully, FIIS needs to become more actively engaged in the marine resource management issues as they affect all of GSB and adjacent New York waters. There are unique opportunities for FIIS to take a leadership role in reaching out cooperatively to government agencies and non-government organizations to encourage a more active approach to the restoration of GSB, as well as increasing public awareness of coastal zone management issues.

Specific Recommendations

<u>Habitat Protection Recommendations</u>

Given the transboundary nature of living marine resources, the National Park Service, occupying much of the southern borders of Great South Bay and Moriches Bay, has an extraordinary opportunity to contribute to the conservation, protection, and, if necessary, restoration of estuarine LMR's.

<u>Potential threats to LMR habitat in the Park</u> - - Among the agencies with LMR or LMR habitat responsibilities and missions noted above, there is strong support for the LMR element of the GMP to address human activities in and around the Park that could potentially impact fishery resources through habitat or water quality impacts. Among the activities most commonly cited as potentially problematic, and discussed during the March 2004 meeting of agency and non-government organization representatives, are the following:

1. party boat benthic disturbance (fishing sinkers)
2. shellfishing benthic disturbance (scraping/ raking//dredging)
3. boating (anchor dredging)
4. personal watercraft (physical disturbance to SAV/tidal marsh habitats)
5. shoreline hardening & dock impacts on intertidal and salt marsh habitats
6. beach nourishment/beach/marsh island creation
7. invasive & introduced nuisance species (*Ulva, Phragmites, Hemigrapsus,*)
8. mosquito control activities
9. water quality

To date, little research has been conducted that would document whether, in fact, any of the above activities presently pose a threat to the condition of LMR habitats within FIIS. NPS is already performing something of an experiment in human activity restriction with its present ban on the use of personal watercraft (PWC) within the Park. This is the third year of this ban and SAV and salt marsh communities are being monitored in selected areas of the Seashore to determine whether the ban on PWC's has had a detectable impact on the extent and condition of these critical LMR habitats.

<u>Habitat Needs Assessment</u> - - A LMR habitat restoration needs assessment should be conducted for FIIS to determine the extent and condition of various habitat types within the Park, and identify impaired areas where restoration efforts should be concentrated. This has already been done, at least in part, for salt marshes. This assessment should be done in close cooperation with state and county agencies, local towns, the SSER Office, and others.

Shellfish Conservation Recommendations

Molluscan populations within GSB and Moriches Bay no longer support large-scale commercially or recreationally viable fisheries. The loss of large suspension-feeding animals such as oysters and hard clams has probably had ecosystem-level effects on environmental characteristics in the bays such as water turbidity, nutrient regeneration, and plankton dynamics (Newell 2004). Recent research supported by New York Sea Grant's Hard Clam Initiative suggest that hard clams, in particular, may not recover substantially on their own without some help in the form of stock enhancement. FIIS should consider participating with other government and non-governmental agencies in hard clam restoration techniques such as seed planting and spawner sanctuaries. Current NPS regulations nominally ban hard clam seed planting within the Park as a prohibited, "…introduction of wildlife." The establishment of hard clam spawner sanctuaries within FIIS is a logical role for NPS with regard to habitat restoration in Great South Bay. Benefits derived from shellfish restoration activities would be system-wide.

Blue crab stocks in the south shore bays are variable, probably because Long Island is at the northern edge of this species' geographic range (SSER 1999). With the loss of other shellfish species, however, blue crabs are becoming a more important commercial and recreational species. Ryer et al. (1990) identified eelgrass beds, macroalgae, and marsh creeks in the Chesapeake Bay as important nursery grounds for juveniles and molting crabs. It is likely these habitats play the same role in Long Island waters. It is recommended that FIIS review management steps being taken to protect existing seagrass and marsh areas and verify that they are compatible with the functioning of these areas as blue crab nursery grounds. This is especially important for seagrass beds, because a larger proportion of the seagrasses in GSB and Moriches Bay are found within the boundaries of FIIS (Bokuniewicz et al. 1993).

The majority of New York's commercial harvest of horseshoe crabs comes from Long Island's South Shore Bay. Landings data do not allow an apportionment of the total catch between these several bays, but it is believed that Great South Bay and Moriches Bay support the most extensive fisheries for these species (K. McKown, NYSDEC, pers. comm. 2005). The importance of intertidal sand flats on the Fire Island side of eastern GSB as a principal spawning area for horseshoe crabs needs to be assessed and NYSDEC is examining this as part of an Island-wide survey of horseshoe crab breeding sites.

No other shellfish species (e.g., oysters, mussels, rock crabs, spider crabs) occurring within FIIS support more than modest commercial or recreational fisheries. None are extensive enough to justify immediate FIIS involvement in their conservation or management.

Finfish Habitat Conservation

As previously stated, commercial fishing anywhere within FIIS is presently prohibited, although it may be occurring. To minimize human impacts, there may be reason to designate certain areas of the park as wilderness or natural zones where recreational finfish harvesting is also prohibited. Consistent with the park's mission and objectives, recreational fishing in other areas of the park should be encouraged. Where recreational fishing is allowed, size and bag limits should be consistent with those established by NYS DEC for all the marine waters of New York State. Given the paucity of documented information about fishing in the park, NPS should conduct studies to determine the current extent of commercial and recreational fishing within FIIS.

Research and Monitoring Recommendations

Very few of the natural resource studies reviewed in this document were conducted within the boundaries of FIIS. Much of the information presented was extrapolated from other studies conducted outside the FIIS boundaries. Data gaps are large enough to suggest that an accurate and comprehensive characterization of the finfish, shellfish, and benthic resources within FIIS is required before the complete nature and extent of FIIS management needs can be identified. Since the FIIS extends much of the length of GSB and part of Moriches Bay and includes a wide variety of habitats, the Park Service is also in an ideal position to implement an annual monitoring program involving water, benthos, and nekton sampling that could track and assess the health of the south shore bays. The NPS, through the Northeast Coastal and Barrier Network program, is engaged in estuarine water quality monitoring and is beginning routine monitoring of salt marsh vegetation and nekton; however, a more comprehensive focus on estuarine and ocean resources may be warranted. Characterization and monitoring studies could, for example, clarify the importance of vegetated habitats within FIIS as nursery grounds for fish and shellfish. They could also provide a fisheries-independent source of information on economically important species and establish baselines for assessing the impacts of environmental changes (Bokuniewicz et al. 1993).

The proximity of the Otis Pike High Dune Wilderness Area to estuarine habitats in Great South Bay provides a unique opportunity to foster research to evaluate the impact of human disturbances on living marine resources. The present wilderness area is terrestrial and is managed to limit vehicle use and other human activities. Extension of the wilderness concept to adjacent intertidal and subtidal bottomlands would produce areas with both minimal marine- and land-based human activities. Creation of a Research Natural Area in accordance with NPS Management Policies (2001) would stimulate science and promote greater understanding of habitat processes and functions, while at the same time restoring and preserving sensitive habitats. In such a protected area, certain activities and disturbances (power boating, anchoring, dredging, fishing, and shellfish harvesting) would be banned. Less intrusive activities, such as sailing and kayaking, might continue. Research might focus on sessile species such as hard clams and finfish species that occur in shallow water and have distinct habitat preferences, such as killifish and silversides. To be effective, activity exclusion and research would need to be conducted on a long-term basis (e.g., decadal time scale) to allow areas to return to an undisturbed state. Discussions with other agencies indicate probable support for the enlargement of the current wilderness concept into tidal waters. NPS should, through the GMP development process, discuss this issue with NYSDEC and the Town of Brookhaven.

The large underwater lands now owned by The Nature Conservancy in Great South Bay are contiguous with FIIS. This juxtaposition may also offer an ideal opportunity to jointly develop a special management area for the purpose of controlling and assessing the impacts of human activities on these shallow, biologically productive marine embayments and their habitats.

The physical layout of FIIS with discrete, high-density communities adjacent to undeveloped areas also provides an opportunity to examine the impact of coastal development on living marine resources. Fishery related issues that could potentially be assessed by comparing developed and undeveloped areas include the environmental and water quality impacts of: 1) docks, bulkheads, and other shore hardening structures; 2) septic systems; and 3) boating activities, including the effects of discharges and channel dredging.

Public Education Recommendations

One of the most important roles that FIIS can play in terms of marine resource management is in public education. The diversity of marine resources and habitats found within the boundaries of the Park and the large number of visitors attracted to the Seashore each year offer a number of possibilities for innovative and engaging public education and outreach programs, beyond the existing programs fielded by the Seashore. Some examples include:

1. An annual "bio-blitz"or short, intensive field census of marine organisms; this could be led by Park staff or contractors, but would involve members of the general public. Such programs have become popular recently and are an effective means of both surveying and documenting the distribution and abundance of LMR's and other flora and fauna in the Park, as well as a means of developing a greater awareness and sensitivity on the part of the public to the need to understand, preserve, and protect the Park's natural resources.

2. Guided snorkeling and/or canoeing field trips to, especially, the shallow tidal waters lying on the bay side of FIIS; these areas are largely inaccessible to boat traffic and contain some of the Park's most undisturbed habitats.

3. Visitor Center. The Park's Visitor Centers at Smith Point, Watch Hill, Sailor's Haven and Patchogue should provide a variety of engaging and informative exhibits about the natural features that together make up the shallow bar-built estuarine embayments along Long Island's South Shore as well as the living marine resources endemic to these systems.

LITERATURE CITED

Able, K. W., R.E. Matheson, W.W. Morse, M.P. Fahay, and G. Sheperd. 1989. Patterns of summer flounder *Paralichthys dentatus* early life history in the mid-Atlantic Bight and New Jersey estuaries. Fisheries Bulletin 88:1-12.

Bokuniewicz, H., A. McElroy, C. Schlenk, and J. Tanski. 1993. Estuarine Resources of the Fire Island National Seashore and Vicinity. Report number NYSGI-T-92-001. New York Sea Grant Institute, Stony Brook, NY. 79 pp. (plus appendices).

Briggs, P.T. 1962. The sport fisheries of Great South Bay and vicinity. N.Y. Fish Game Journal 9(1):1-36.

_____ and J.S. O'Connor. 1971. Comparison of shore-zone fishes over naturally vegetated and sand-filled bottoms in the Great South Bay. N.Y. Fish Game Journal 18:15-41.

Buckner, S.C. 1984. Aspects of the Population Dynamics of the Hard Clam, *Mercenaria mercenaria*, in Great South Bay, NY. Ph.D. thesis. Marine Sciences Research Center, State University of New York, Stony Brook, New York. 217 pp.

Bulger, A.J., B.P. Hayden, M.G. McCormick-Ray, M.E. Monaco, and D.M. Nelson. 1990. A proposed estuarine classification: analysis of species salinity ranges. ELMR Rept. No. 5 Strategic Assessment Branch, NOS/NOAA. Rockville, MD. 28 p.

Burger, J. and W.A. Montevecchi. 1975. Tidal synchronization and nest selection in the northern diamondback terrapin, *Malaclemys terrapin terrapin* Scheopff. Copeia 1975: 113-119.

Castro, L.R. and R.K. Cowen. 1991. Environmental factors affecting the early life history of bay anchovy *Anchoa mitchilli* in Great South Bay, New York. Marine Ecology Progress Series 76: 235-247.

Cerrato, R.M. 1983. Benthic Borrow Area Investigations, South Shore of Long Island, New York. Marine Sciences Research Center. Special Report No. 51. State University of New York, Stony Brook, New York. 654 pp.

_____. 1986. A Seasonal Study of the Benthic Fauna in Moriches Bay. Marine Sciences Research Center. Special Report No. 72. State University of New York, Stony Brook, New York. 160 pp.

Conover, D.O. and S.A. Murawski. 1982. Offshore winter migration of the Atlantic silverside *Menidia menidia*. Fisheries Bulletin 80: 145-149.

COSMA. 1985. Suffolk County's Hard Clam Industry: An Overview and Analysis of Management Alternatives. Report by the Coastal Ocean Science and Management Alternatives

(COSMA) Program, Marine Sciences Research Center, State University of New York at Stony Brook, Spec. Rept. 63.

Croker, R.A. 1970. Intertidal sand macrofauna from Long Island, NY. Chesapeake Science 11: 134-137.

Grosslein, M.D. and T.R. Azarovitz. 1982. Fish distribution. MESA New York Bight Atlas Monograph 15. New York Sea Grant Institute. 182 p.

Grover, J.J. 1982. The comparative feeding ecology of five, inshore marine fishes off Long Island, New York. Ph.D. dissertation. Rutgers Univ., New Brunswick, N.J.

Hanlon, J.R. 1983. Fish and wildlife resource studies for the Fire Island Inlet to Montauk Point, New York, beach erosion control and hurricane protection project reformulation study, estuarine resource component. U.S. Dept. Interior, Fish and Wildl. Serv. , Region 5, Upton, N.Y. 44 p., 9 appendices.

Juanes, F. 1992. The advantages of advection: recruitment, piscivory, growth, and consumption of young-of-the-year bluefish (Pomatomus saltatrix). Ph.D. dissertation, State University of New York, Stony Brook. 187 p.

Kassner, J, R. Cerrato, and T. Carrano. 1991. Towards Understanding and Improving the Abundance of Hard Clams (*Mercenaria mercenaria*) in the Eastern Great South Bay, N.Y. *In:* Proceedings of the First Rhode Island Shellfisheries Conference. Edited by M.A. Rice, M. Grady, and M.A. Schwartz. Rhode Island Sea Grant, University of Rhode Island Bay Campus, Narragansett. pp 69-78.

Kneib, R.T. 1986. The role of *Fundulus heteroclitus* in salt marsh trophic dynamics. American Zoologist 26:259-269.

Larson, A. A. 2000. The Role of Substrate Type in Characterizing Community Parameters and the Distribution of *Mercenaria mercenaria* (L.) in Great South Bay. M.S. thesis. Marine Sciences Research Center, State University of New York, Stony Brook, New York.

Marine Sciences Research Center. 1973. Final Report of the Oceanographic and Biological Study for Southwest Sewer District #3, Suffolk County, NY. Prepared for Bowe, Walsh and Associates, Huntington Station, NY by the Marine Sciences Research Center, State University of New York, Stony Brook, New York. 629 pp.

Merriner, J.V. 1975. Food habits of the weakfish, *Cynoscion regalis*, in North Carolina waters. Chesapeake Science 16:74-76.

Miller, D. 1977. Ichthyoplankton of Great South Bay, New York. M.S. thesis, Adelphi Univ. 66 p.

Monteleone, D.M. 1992. Seasonality and abundance of ichthyoplankton in Great South Bay, New York. Estuaries 15:230-238.

National Park Service. 2003. Fire Island National Seashore Short-Term Community Storm Surge Protection Plan Environmental Assessment. National Park Service, Patchogue, NY 145 pp.

_____. 2003. 2003 Annual Report of the Fire Island National Seashore. *Soundings* Vol. 1, No. 1. 19 pp.

Newell, R.I.E. 2004. Ecosystem influences of natural and cultivated populations of suspension-feeding bivalve mollusks: A review. Journal of Shellfish 23: 51-61.

NY State Department of Environmental Conservation 2002. 2002 Atlantic Ocean Surfclam Population Assessment. NY State Department of Environmental Conservation, Bureau of Marine Resources, East Setauket, NY.

O'Connor, J.S. 1972. The benthic macrofauna of Moriches Bay, NY. Biological Bulletin 142: 84-102.

Olla, B.L., A.J. Bejda, and A.D. Martin. 1975. Activity, movements, and feeding behavior of the cunner, *Tautogolabrus adspersus*, and comparison of food habits with young tautog, *Tautoga onitis*, off Long Island, New York. Fisheries Bulletin 73:895-900.

Olla, B.L., R. Wicklund, and S. Wilk. 1969. Behavior of winter flounder in a natural habitat. Transactions of the American Fisheries Society 98:717-720.

Poole, J.C. 1961. Age and growth of the fluke population of Great South Bay and their significance to the sport fishery. N.Y. Fish Game Journal 8:1-18.

_____. 1962. The fluke population of Great South Bay in relation to the sport fishery. New York Fish Game Journal 9:93-117.

_____. 1964. Feeding habits of the summer flounder in Great South Bay. New York Fish Game Journal 11:28-34.

Raposa, K.B. and C.A. Oviatt. 2000. The influence of contiguous shoreline type, distance from shore, and vegetation biomass on nekton community structure in eelgrass beds. Estuaries 23: 46-55.

Roundtree, R.A. and K.W. Able. 1992. Fauna of polyhaline subtidal marsh creeks in southern New Jersey: composition, abundance and biomass. Estuaries 15: 171-185.

Ryer, C., J. van Monfrans, and R. Orth. 1990. Utilization of seagrass meadow and tidal marsh creek by blue crabs *Callinectes sapidus*. II. Spatial and temporal patterns of molting. Bulletin of Marine Science 46: 95-104.

Schaefer, R.H. 1967. Species composition, size and seasonal abundance of fish in the surf waters of Long Island. New York Fish and Game Journal 14(1): 1-46.

_____. 1970. Feeding habits of striped bass from the surf waters of Long Island. New York Fish Game Journal 17:1-17.

Shima, M. and R.K. Cowen. 1989. Potential change in the distribution of larval fish within Great South Bay, New York in response to recurrent phytoplankton blooms. pp. 599-624 in Cosper, E.M., V.M. Bricelj, and E.J. Carpenter (eds.) Novel Phytoplankton Blooms. Springer-Verlag, New York.

SSER 1999. Crustacean Shellfish. South Shore Estuary Reserve Technical Report. NY Department of State, Division of Coastal Resources, Albany, NY. 23 pp.

Steadman, G. 1999. Embayment Use Study of the South Shore Estuary Reserve Comprehensive Management Plan. Final Report. Prepared for South Shore Estuary Reserve Council and New York State Department of State, Division of Coastal Resources.

Steinback, J.M.K. 1999. The Ocean Beach Invertebrates of Fire Island National Seashore, New York: Spatial and Temporal Trends and the Effects of Vehicular Disturbance. M.S. thesis. Marine Sciences Research Center, State University of New York, Stony Brook, New York. 252 pp.

Taylor, M.H. and L. DiMichele. 1983. Sapwning site utilization in a Delaware population of *Fundulus heteroclitus* (Pices: Cypriniodontidae). Copeia 1983: 719-725.

U.S. Army Corps of Engineers 2004. Fire Island Inlet to Montauk Point Reformulation Study Borrow Area Database. NY District, Environmental Analysis Branch, US Army Corps of Engineers, New York

WAPORA. 1982. Impact Assessment on Shellfish Resources of Great South Bay, South Oyster Bay, and Hempstead Bay, NY. Draft report submitted to U.S. Environmental Protection Agency, Region II, New York, NY by WAPORA, Inc.

Wiggins, M.H. 1986. Differences in Benthic Fauna between Polluted and Unpolluted Areas as Based on Coliform Concentration. M.S. thesis. Marine Sciences Research Center, State University of New York, Stony Brook, New York. 214 pp.

NPS D-127 December 2005